# A Flame on the Front Line

## Journey from America to Afghanistan

## John Weaver

# Dedication

To all the "flames" who have walked the halls of Free Will Baptist Bible College. As Steve Green sings, "May all who come behind us find us faithful. May the fire of our devotion light their way. May the footprints that we leave, lead them to believe, and the lives we live inspire them to obey."

# Acknowledgments

I am indebted to numerous people around the world for making another dream come true. The scope of this journey spans cities, countries and continents, so to remember everyone would fill the pages of another book. A special thanks to: my loving family; faithful friends who have inspired me to follow God's call to Afghanistan; the many fellowships that have supported me; FWBBC for a wonderful foundation; FWB-IMB for sending me on my first trip in 1990; CIU faculty; TSC staff; our Shelter Now Team; Xulon Press; and most of all, my Loving Heavenly Father for creating me and calling me to join Him on this great adventure of knowing Him and making Him known.

# Contents

Introduction ............................................... vi

Chapter 1: The Lion is Dead ................................ 10

Chapter 2: Dawning ........................................ 19

Chapter 3: Happy Hoodlums .............................. 29

Chapter 4: Reality Check .................................. 42

Chapter 5: Step by Step .................................. 52

Chapter 6: Found: FWBBC ............................... 64

Chapter 7: Goen Hall ..................................... 83

Chapter 8: Live and Learn ............................... 100

Chapter 9: Regions Beyond ............................... 122

Chapter 10: Go Home… ................................. 136

Chapter 11: Answering Abdullah ....................... 145

# Introduction

It was July 4, 2009 — two hundred and thirty years since America's founding fathers wrote, "We hold these truths to be self-evident, that all men are created equal, that they are endowed by their Creator with certain inalienable Rights, that among these are Life, Liberty and the pursuit of Happiness." I was busy writing similar inspiring statements. The story has been lived. The cast of characters is complete. Now that I have received some pertinent suggestions from a friend, the final manuscript will soon be ready.

Meanwhile, the population of our planet passed 6 ½ billion and the media was reporting events around the world. Millions were mourning the death of the legendary Michael Jackson, the Statue of Liberty's crown was open again for the first time since 9/11, U.S. military forces were still pursuing the Taliban as Afghanistan's presidential elections approached, Swiss tennis champion Roger Federer was on the verge of a world record in Wimbledon, and President

Obama was making history with Russian leaders in Moscow.

Since 2000, I've had the privilege of being a small part of history inside Afghanistan by living and working there. On top of that, I've had numerous opportunities to travel around the world and speak about it. If you read my first book *Inside Afghanistan*, you will enjoy how this book explores new territory of the work and journey from America to Afghanistan. Many pages about this part of the planet are still being written. For me personally, there are still many stories to tell about being a "flame on the front line" in the land of my dreams.

The humanitarian service of both our Christian organization and the international community continues to touch millions of lives inside Afghanistan. Whole communities are being transformed. Throughout the country we see economic opportunities and small businesses springing up. Countless boys and girls are back in school. Thousands of young men and women are studying at various institutes and universities, learning English and computer skills and preparing for the future of their beloved homeland. ISAF, the International Security Armed Forces, is not only helping to maintain peace and administer justice, but also equipping the Afghan National Army and Police force. There are so many more meaningful stories than those of suicide bombers inside Afghanistan.

I still love this unique line of practical work. I am also grateful to be writing again, mostly from the Land of the Afghans. I feel blessed because I've experienced both writing and working as a single and, now, as a married person. In spite of the challenges, dangers and risks, Afghanistan has treated me well over the years. Guess what! I met the most beautiful woman in the world there...but this is a story for another book. I just wanted to illustrate that not everything or everyone inside Afghanistan is evil.

Will you embark on this expedition with me? It is a long road stretching from Northern Virginia to Northern Afghanistan. The travels contain episodes of faith and family, opportunity and obedience, pain and preparation, failure and fulfillment, disappointment and destiny. I am grateful for the privilege of testifying to how God's Sovereign Hand has guided and provided. I wanted to put some of it down on paper as a stone of remembrance. This is my hope as we trek through these pages together:

1) That our understanding of God's greatness, love, faithfulness, and sovereign work in the world will be enlarged to a more God-sized view;

2) That we will take up the challenge to passionately pursue God's kingdom, practice mercy, love justice, and walk humbly with the Lord our God;

3) That our worldview, especially toward Muslims, will become more balanced and some of our attitudes or responses will be more compassionate;

4) That our love for our country will be deepened and focused by seeing more clearly the neces-

sity of our ultimate allegiance to God and our eternal home.

Welcome aboard an adventurous journey, or *khush omaded*, as my Afghan friends would say. As you read on, may you be encouraged as a "flame on your front line," and may some of your questions about Afghanistan and Islam be addressed. God be with you! *Bon voyage!*

# Chapter 1

# The Lion Is Dead

Almost overnight a dry and dusty tiny town in Takhar was transformed into a media head-quarters. It was hard for reporters to access this area because of the civil war inside Afghanistan. The rugged terrain, lack of road system and absence of phone or power lines made it even more difficult. Those who made the challenging journey had to cross the border from Tajikistan. Most arrived unannounced in search of the story about the possible savior of Afghanistan.

The legendary leader of the Northern Alliance, General Ahmad Shah Massoud, was the target of a Taliban terrorist attack. During the 1980s he earned the nickname, Lion of Panjshir, as he led the famed Mujahidin guerilla fighters against the Soviets. He not only survived Stalin's invasion; he harassed and decimated the Russian forces until they withdrew from Afghanistan in 1989. Today, my journal entry reads September 10, 2001 and many now believe the Lion is dead.

The tyranny of the Taliban almost engulfed Afghanistan. The Taliban were on the verge of taking control of the entire country. Their hope was to wrap things up before the long, cold winter season that would shortly come. Soon the Land of the Afghans would serve as a base of operations for the Taliban and al-Qaeda's worldwide mission of religious conquest. Only a small corner of the country remained in the hands of the Northern Alliance, mostly due to the unifying leadership and military mind of General Massoud.

This is why two Arab-Africans, disguised as journalists, were drinking tea with the infamous warlord the morning called 9/9. The Lion loved to entertain reporters, because they told the world about the cruelty of the Taliban. Today, however, their goal was to get close enough to clandestinely kill him. If the two suicide bombers succeeded in snuffing out the life of the "invincible Lion of the Panjshir," it would only be a matter of days before the entire country would be in Taliban hands. The result would be chaos, massacres and killing fields, as they would ruthlessly rule everything and everyone in Afghanistan.

As the media was making its way to Afghanistan, other terrible terrorist attacks were lurking in the darkness. Again, the Taliban and its al-Qaeda networks were coordinating and creating a wicked plan of action. This time suicide bombers would come in the form of airplanes, hijacked by hellish men to wreak havoc on New York City, Washington, D.C., and only God knows what other places. Soon, the whole world would be watching some of the worst terrorist attacks in history.

The media that had not already mobilized because of Massoud's death moved immediately toward Afghanistan. Indeed, our world was rocked by 9/11. We were all affected, for we all felt it in some manner. It altered our agendas. Yes, 9/11 changed our lives and opened our curiosity to the world of Islam, leaving us with more questions than answers. It put Afghanistan on our map. It mobilized our U.S. Armed Forces, who never imagined they would spend Christmas of 2001 in such a strange, snowy, mountainous land. The staffs of *The New Yorker*, CNN, *The Boston Globe* and ABC News never dreamed of going to the Land of the Afghans before the hellish terrorist attacks.

## Unexpected Discovery

The media and the military never anticipated meeting a long-bearded, Afghan-looking American in Northern Afghanistan. It was an astonishing moment for them. Nor did I ever imagine having to evacuate from the land of my dreams because of 9/9 or 9/11. To their surprise, I was not only a Westerner in a war zone, but an American actively serving the sworn enemies of the Taliban. They all wondered, "How did he get here and why was he so passionate about serving the war-torn people of Afghanistan?"

I was born in Washington, D.C., and grew up mostly in Northern Virginia. Although both of my grandfathers fought faithfully in World War II, and one of my grandmothers worked at the Pentagon while my Grandfather Hoover was overseas, I never wore a uniform. My father did in the Navy, as well as an older brother who joined the Air Force after high school. But my desire to work in Afghanistan is more about divine destiny, which is not necessarily related to the Department of Defense or the world of media.

I did not go to Afghanistan as a volunteer for a faith-based relief and development organization to get rich or become famous. Instead of an expensive media budget or a quick military airlift, my journey from America to Afghanistan was more like a long roller coaster ride of trials and painful preparation before finally arriving. While I am grateful for the devoted service of our military and the media's dedication to report the news of our world, I arrived with neither gun nor camera. In fact, we did not even have cell phones back then. All I had was a Bible, a journal and a change of clothes in my backpack. I endured the long expedition, by the grace of God, to lay down my life in the service of others.

I moved into Northern Afghanistan in the summer of 2000. It was a match made in heaven. I fell in love with the place and the people; however, it wasn't always easy being a Christian American, doing relief work in the Islamic country. We were the only ones serving the suffering in that area, yet I was threatened many times. At one food distribution point an Afghan Muslim man even tried to kill me. But God protected me and allowed our organization to do much good for the war-torn people. Often I felt like Winston Churchill, who, during World War II, spoke about stepping into destiny and how all his life had been preparation for this hour and trial. Sometimes we have those divine moments or sovereign seasons, where we sense "for such a time as this I have entered the kingdom."

By the time Afghanistan made the news after General Massoud's assassination on 9/9 and the terrorist attacks of 9/11, we were already helping thousands of internally displaced Afghan families. Almost all of our beneficiaries were homeless, because the Taliban had forcefully invaded their villages and burned their homes. They were the lucky ones, who escaped, fleeing the fires to survive. Christian organizations had been in the region serving Afghans for over 50 years. I was just a rookie who recently arrived on the scene to implement million-dollar USAID projects from our little four-room mud house. In addition, as the main partner for the World Food Program (WFP) in the area, we distributed tons of wheat to the poor and as payment to thousands of men in our Food for Work programs.

Our relief and development services were designed to improve their overall quality of life. It is all about life. God has so blessed my life that it comes natural to want to help others. It is a privilege to serve the poorest of the poor, especially those who are in danger or who have suffered so much destruction. When people talked about leaving for safer zones, I just smiled. I had been living peacefully in the middle of a war zone, doing God's work, before the terrorism of Afghanistan reached my homeland.

Living as a "flame on the front line" was a dream come true. Since finishing college, I had an inner conviction that I would one day be inside Afghanistan. The thought of having to leave Afghanistan crushed me. All around me, people were suffering. We had been called to assist them. Danger drives some away, but it draws others like a magnet to help the hurting. I do not deliberately go looking for danger, but I don't think we have to always run from it. So after 9/11, when I was presented with the possibility of continuing our mission of mercy inside Afghanistan, I gladly rose to the challenge.

By the end of September 2001, many more were preparing for another challenge. It would be multi-faceted. For some, their time and energy would be consumed in writing, reporting, taking photos, and interviewing on a media mission for the western world. Others would leave on planes, ships and submarines on a mission of justice in the new war against terrorism.

When I first realized this I didn't know how to respond. As I heard a knock on our office door a few weeks after the terrorist attacks, I was unaware of the surprise before me. Opening the door, I saw another American, John, from *The New Yorker*. I cannot remember which of us was more shocked. I didn't know that the Americans had already arrived, and he had been told all the Americans and other foreigners had left Afghanistan.

Our divine appointment was the dawn of a discovery, a success story if you will. Soon our humanitarian projects in Northern Afghanistan would be part of the media's message. First, *The New Yorker*, then *The Boston Globe* and various newspapers in

North Carolina reported our work and my presence in Northern Afghanistan. Soon after, I was seen all over the globe, featured on ABC Nightly News with Peter Jennings and CNN with Saira Shah. Here is a sample of what was being said at that time:

> "After September 11, when the political situation became too dangerous, the aid groups pulled their international staffs out of the country. One worker chose to stay…The people who live there have accepted John Weaver as a friend and ally." *–The New Yorker.*

> "Hundreds of refugees, ragged images silhouetted by the dust, gathered yesterday outside the large wooden doors….What much of the world is seeing for the first time is nothing new to John Weaver." *–The Boston Globe.*

> "I saw John Weaver for the first time in October 2001 on ABC News. When John's face appeared on the screen, I knew there was something special about him. I could see it in his eyes, his smile, and his interaction with the Afghan people. To me, John is a modern-day Good Samaritan. He truly models that the greatest in the world is the one who serves, which sometimes means helping the poorest of the poor in very difficult and dangerous settings."—Franklin Graham, President of

Samaritan's Purse and the Billy Graham
Evangelistic Association (BGEA).

"John Weaver impressed me and my team
as a rare example of true selflessness. His
humanity, humor, and courage shine out
as testaments to the triumph of the human
spirit." –Saira Shah, reporter for CNN docu-
mentaries *Beneath the Veil* and *Unholy War*.

The sound bites were juicy. My team and I were
helping the hated enemies of the Taliban. Immediate
danger surrounded us daily. We were living on the
front line in the face of terror. I may have been the
only active American relief worker there at that time.
A stream of journalists had arrived and a calvary of
soldiers was coming. The only other two Americans
in the country were Heather Mercer and Dayna Curry,
who worked in Kabul. They were imprisoned by the
Taliban, along with six other expatriate colleagues
and sixteen local Afghan staff. They all survived as
*Prisoners of Hope*. The other book about their experience is *Escape from Kabul*.

It was an overwhelming feeling being there in
those tense days serving the people I have come
to love so much. It doesn't matter if I was the only
American or not. That is where God in His sovereignty planted me. Our humanitarian success story is
simply about trust and obedience. We believed in the
goodness of God and allowed Him to use us for His
good purposes. As Wayne Watson sings, "For such a
time as this I was placed upon the earth, to hear the

voice of God and do His will whatever it is." His will was to work with all my might to serve those suffering the most. There were times, however, when I wondered, "What in the world am I doing here?" And many others around the world were asking a similar question, "How did this young man make the journey from America to Afghanistan?"

# Chapter 2

# Dawning

While serving in the Philippines in 1997, God gave me a vivid vision of Afghanistan. I have told this story many times in response to the question, "How did you get to Afghanistan?" But I am not sure if this is really the dawning of the journey. Where did it all begin? Some might say in the belly of my wonderful mother, Sandra Virginia Weaver. Perhaps the journey to Afghanistan did start and a plan was set in motion at some divine meeting in my mother's womb.

I say this with a smile for two reasons. First, it is a God thing. The Bible says: "You made all the delicate, inner parts of my body and knit me together in my mother's womb. Thank you for making me so wonderfully complex! Your workmanship is marvelous—how well I know it. You watched me as I was being formed in utter seclusion, as I was woven together in the dark of the womb. You saw me before

I was born. Every day of my life was recorded in your book. Every moment was laid out before a single day had passed. How precious are your thoughts about me, O God. They cannot be numbered!" (Psalm 139:13–16). God's word paints the picture that He has us in view while we are all developing those first nine months. It is His hands that are forming us and shaping us to be the people we become at the miraculous moment we call birth.

Second, it is a family affair. My mother tells me I was so eager to come into the world that she almost delivered me in an elevator. That would have been an unusual experience. Imagine the headline: Baby Delivered Between 3rd and 4th Floors of George Washington Hospital! Pondering on that possibility, points to the fact that I've always been anxious to go where no one has gone before! An apostolic attitude, pioneering personality or love for the unknown began to flame before I was placed in the cradle at my Northern Virginian home, around Valentine's Day of 1970. At this time in history there were some interesting events taking place inside Afghanistan. God's sovereignty had already led many flames to burn in the Land of the Afghans that I hope we will meet in the future.

### Before the Foundations

If we probe the question of how I ended up in Afghanistan, there is a dynamic truth to be discovered. My trek to the ends of the earth was planned before my father, Jerry Weaver, Sr., ever dreamed of naming a son after his own father, John Mack

Weaver, Jr. In the eternal view, I was seen in Northern Afghanistan before my parents ever saw each other in Northern Virginia.

Although I have said several times, "I am neither prophet nor the son of a prophet," there is a prophetic verse that is profound and very personal to me. The Lord Almighty said to the prophet Jeremiah several thousands of years ago, "I knew you before I formed you in your mother's womb. Before you were born I set you apart and appointed you as my prophet to the nations." (Jeremiah 1:5).

I believe in God's foreknowledge and the free will of man. It is sometimes hard to reconcile these two concepts. I am a graduate of Free Will Baptist Bible College (FWBBC). You will learn more about this seemingly ironic expression as you keep reading. Some of my favorite phrases are "God is sovereign" and "the Hand of Providence." On the other hand, especially working in Afghanistan, sometimes we have to make on-the-spot decisions and make the most of the opportunity. Yes, we pray and seek the face of God, but often the choice is up to us. Many times I have told our team in Afghanistan "Go for it" or "Just do it," because we are co-laborers with God. Sometimes by simply asking, "What do you think we should do?" the Spirit of God has helped us use our free-will faculties to find the mind of Christ and respond to the glory of God and the good of others.

Often, in terms of salvation, I have wrestled with this issue of predestination and people's choices with life. One word picture has helped me balance the dichotomy. Imagine a door. Remember the Messiah said, "I am the door, those who enter are saved." The door is labeled, "Whosoever." For the Bible says, "Whosoever calls upon the name of the Lord will be saved." We believe Jesus is the Lamb of God, who takes away the sins of the world. For God so loved the world that He sent Jesus to die for all. Jesus is the atoning sacrifice for the sins of all people. Therefore, the invitation is for *everyone*. Now, look at the other side of the door and read, "Elect." This means that "whosoever" enters through Jesus, the only door of salvation, becomes God's chosen son or daughter. On the other side of the door, we are God's beloved family or His elect!

My favorite book in the New Testament is Ephesians. I fell in love with it so much that I memorized all six chapters while studying at FWBBC. A few phrases from it illustrate truth that is beyond comprehension, yet basic Christian realism: "All praise to God, the Father of our Lord Jesus Christ, who has blessed us with every spiritual blessing in the heavenly realms because we are united with Christ. Even before he made the world, God loved us and chose us in Christ to be holy and without fault in his eyes. God decided in advance to adopt us into his own family by bringing us to himself through Jesus Christ. This is what he wanted to do, and it gave him great pleasure. So we praise God for the glorious grace he has poured out on us who belong to his dear Son. He is so rich in kindness and grace that he purchased our freedom with the blood of his Son and forgave our sins." (Ephesians 1:3-7).

**Chief of Sinners**

Even though I didn't know it at the time, my journey to Northern Afghanistan started the day I decided to follow the Lord Jesus Christ, the Way, the Truth and the Life. Until then my life had a different direction and final destination. The message of the Messiah is that as the Father sent me, now I send you. If we know the Son of God, then we should know that we are sent ones, just as the Father sent the Son from heaven to earth. We are all on a mission, but most of us miss this. I was born in Washington, D.C., the capital of the blessed land we call America, yet my childhood was void of our spiritual heritage. I grew up in Northern Virginia, the youngest of three sons, not knowing about the faith of some our founding fathers.

Our home was not "hell on earth" but it was far from "Thy will be done on Earth as it is in Heaven." We had some worldly possessions, but lacked reality in our lives. I was neither a neglected nor an abandoned child. I never tasted the pain of physical abuse. I did, however, personally experiment with the chemistry of bad behavior, most of it learned at home. Some of my childhood memories are sweet and family focused, but I have to dig in the recesses of my mind to retrieve many of them. On the other hand, I remember the frequent fights, family feuds and full range of fleshly entertainment that we all seem to selfishly indulge in and enjoy more than we were willing to admit. The liberty we felt was a license to live anyway we wished. We didn't have a family bumper sticker, but if we did, "*Lust or Bust*" would have been appropriate.

You may soon agree with me that my life is best summarized by these beautiful words found in the Bible: "This is a trustworthy saying, and everyone should accept it: 'Christ Jesus came into the world to save sinners'—and I am the worst of them all. But God had mercy on me so that Christ Jesus could use me as a prime example of His great patience with even the worst sinners. Then others will realize that they, too, can believe in Him and receive eternal life. All honor and glory to God forever and ever! He is the eternal King. Amen." (I Timothy 1:15-17).

My mother tried to promote peace and spread love in our home. She was the glue that held things together, or at least she tried. I do remember her as one who was tough but tender, concerned and very caring. She modeled before us the ways of service and selflessness. Most of time, however, her four men, a workaholic husband and three wild sons were too self-centered to see it. If it had not been for the love I received from my mom, there would probably not be the rest of the story. I was destined for a one-way path of destruction, even suicidal at times. But somehow I was divinely detoured. Mom played a part in this in ways that I would only learn later in life.

**Adventurously Active**
Growing up in Virginia I remember going to drag races with my dad and playing a lot of sports with my brothers. Football and baseball were my favor-

ites. We were raised to love the Washington Redskins and despise the Dallas Cowboys. My dad had a souped-up Volkswagen that gave us a good excuse to spend much time at the drag strip. As passionate and energetic men, we needed various ways to burn off steam. My sport memories are probably the fondest. Quarterback was where the action was for me. I was convinced that one day I'd be the next Joe Montana. I recall a few passes and quarterback sneaks that resulted in seven points.

My brothers called me twinkle toes. I'm not sure if it was my blazing speed or my dancing skills in the pocket. During Little League baseball season, one hot and humid afternoon in Fairfax County, I pulled off a solo triple play. Shortstop was my favorite position. I caught the quick line drive hit my way, tagged the runner who took off from second base, and then whizzed the ball to first base before that runner could return. Wow, I thought for sure Cal Ripken from the Baltimore Orioles would be dropping by to see me any moment.

Our circumstances and the culture around us led us to do more exciting things than just expending energy on the athletic field. Several memories are etched in my mind from our time in Northern Virginia. One is in 1979, when I was only nine years old and my next older brother, Jerry, was turning twelve. As it was at our house, so it was at our friend's house. Adult beverages could be found in cabinets. You didn't need to be a rocket scientist to discover it, nor a brain surgeon to open it. One night, curiosity almost killed us, like a bunch of stray cats lurking for food in a dark alley. It turned out to a dangerous chemistry experiment.

We did the stray-cat strut all right. In fact, it lasted all night. We created our own test tubes of bourbon, beer and other intoxicating beverages. The outcome was just short of an explosion, and one unpleasant memory stands out. I spent several hours in the bathroom after my first bout with beer and brandy. I obviously lost the match and ended up losing my breakfast, lunch and dinner as a result. Later, our friend's parents, who refrained from tearing us apart, told me that I had passed out and slept in the bathtub.

As a child I was full of inquisitiveness and quite an extrovert. Despite the drive to be active and adventurous, there was something deep inside that wanted the simpler side of life. At times, I even searched for "quiet places" to escape the rat race and painful experiences of life. One childhood memory illustrates my introverted side. Imagine with me a massive maple tree leveled flat by the force of a hurricane leaving a huge hole in the ground, because the large root system is now hanging outside the dirt like a giant spider web. Got the picture?

That is where I loved to hang out; in the hole dug out by the uprooted tree. It was a secluded spot, a peaceful place for me. Unfortunately, the saying that has some truth, "like father like son," sometimes got the best of me. Often my secret hideout became a storehouse for alcohol and forbidden viewing material or a manhole from which we could declare war by launching dirt clogs at each other. Sadly, these hidden activities were only a reflection of what was happening inside our house and the secret rooms of our hearts.

## A Burning Bush Experience

On this day we were in a neighbor's yard in Pyromaniac Class 101. Again, curiosity was calling. Our fire lab was just beyond the row of front yard trees in the little concrete drainage area. It's not clear what happened...between our smoking something, shining magnifying glasses, and seeing how leaves burn, our neighbor's bushes began blazing with fire. This was not a Prophet Moses' Burning Bush experience. We were scared to death, not because of God's awesome presence, but because of the consequences of our foolish fire tactics. The fire engines came and water squelched the flames before anyone was hurt or property was severely damaged.

Our fondness for fire began to flame. One afternoon, we made a bomb in our backyard. The experiment took place in our one-room tree house, which nestled 10 feet high in a huge oak tree. Like Jekyl and Hyde, my brother and I felt the need for another crazy Frankenstein-type experiment. Curiosity almost killed us again, as we filled a five-gallon bucket with various flammable chemicals and threw a match in it. The explosion rocked our little world and rang our eardrums. Thankfully, we survived. Our sufferings were only layers of black suet and singed hair. It was as if we had spent some time in Mom's oven, but the smell was not like the delicious cakes or cookies she loved to bake.

Like most American families, we loved to celebrate the Fourth of July. How blessed we are as a nation of democracy, freedom and opportunity. The activities on the Fourth of July illustrate these with an abundance of food and fun, parties and picnics. Then at night almost the entire nation is lit as fireworks soar in the sky. We also loved to make our own fireworks or keep a stash of firecrackers to continue the festivities throughout the year. Homemade concoctions can be deadly, and firecrackers hurt when you play pretend war with them. Later, I remembered these crazy childhood experiences whenever I heard the Taliban rocket attacks that landed near my house during Afghanistan's civil war. Now I recall them at the sound of the frequent suicide bombers inside Afghanistan.

By the way, fire is dangerous and deadly. Please do *not* play with it or attempt any of these foolish things you are reading. These "side bites" and funny stories are only used to demonstrate what kind of person I was and to help illustrate a life that has been changed. If you keep reading you will learn the real reason I refer to myself as a "flame."

# Chapter 3

# Happy Hoodlums

As the third of three sons, my older brothers, Phil and Jerry, probably had as much impact on my early life as my parents did. They were busy parents of the 70s, and three naturally independent boys thrived in good and bad ways under the general lack of supervision in our home. I ended up experimenting with life as my older brothers discovered it. We always sought to experience life in fifth gear, to the fullest. I learned to live everyday as if it were my last, or at least the way I spent my days might cause you to believe that. The truth is I knew nothing about eternity and was afraid of death. When we live each day to the max, however, it is as if we are living like there is no tomorrow. We probably got in about as much trouble as kids can get into without ending up in prison. That was partly because sometimes we didn't get caught.

Being the youngest brother explains why I experienced so much at an early age. We are products of our environment, and our surroundings shape a lot of our approach to and outlook on life. Though most of what I did was only an attempt to imitate what I saw in others, still something inside me wanted the all-out adventure. For example, when school closed because of snow, we would bumper ride all over Northern Virginia.

Bumper riding is the dangerous sport where you sneak behind a car stopped at a stop sign. As the car slowly takes off in the snow or ice, you squat down and grab the bumper of the car. If you can hold on and stay bent down like a baseball catcher, the vehicle will take you to the next stop. For us happy hoodlums it was fun, free transport. On the boring winter days we would walk over to I-95 to throw snowballs at cars. Our thinking was, "Since we are snowbound let's make the most of it." Our creating opportunities based on our settings promoted both healthy and hellish activities. No doubt, developing this redeem-the-time mindset was great preparation for the adventurous life that awaited me in Afghanistan.

**Stealing Santa**

Christmas is an important holiday season full of festivities and plenty of possibilities. One year at this time, a group of us young guys went caroling several times. This singing activity sounds appropriate and innocent. We knew very little about the real meaning of "Hark the Herald Angels Sing" or "Joy to the World the Lord Has Come." We couldn't carry a tune in a bucket; nevertheless we totally enjoyed the experience. This was mostly because it brought unexpected surprises in the form of candy, presents, or even the good green stuff (money). Our hearty attempt to have a good time, however, sometimes got out of control. Temptations could turn the "season to be jolly" sour, and we would act like the Grinch who stole Christmas.

Often, the time for giving caused us to take advantage of people. I guess we were more "naughty" than "nice." Our thinking was that if our audience didn't bless us for our karaoke caroling, we could always steal and reward ourselves. One day, we took this idea to the extreme. It was the week before Christmas and a group of us were casually watching a soccer game, one of the few sports we didn't play. But other things caught our eyes such as ladies purses lying on the ground. Possessed with thoughts of personal gain, one of my buddies snatched a purse from the sidelines and tossed it to me, as if we were playing football. Then they, my friends, took off, as if to block for me. Not knowing what else to do, I followed running with all my might.

**Undercover Police**

Soccer games did not usually draw large crowds, but almost every parent is present watching his or her little "Johnny" play on the field. On this day, there happened to be a secret agent or undercover police in the crowd. Northern Virginia is an area full of military personnel and government employees of all kinds. With one eye this skillful spy watched his son dribble the soccer ball, and with the other eye he witnessed our act of thievery. He began to chase us down like a lion after its prey. I was oblivious to it and hadn't considered that my friends provided no blocking for my back. They were still way out front, when I heard the heavy footsteps bearing down on me. In fear, I looked back and threw the purse down. By then, I knew I couldn't hold out, and he caught up with me.

Somehow my friends picked the right purse. I was soon charged with grand theft, because it contained over $500 in family Christmas money. Fortunately, the juvenile judge had mercy on me when I tearfully apologized and explained the whole ordeal. It was a lesson learned, however, we did not stop stealing. There was still some transformation to take place in my heart and mind.

By the time I was a freshman in high school, my life consisted of trouble and rebellion. I knew a lot more about unholy acts and abusive substances from personal experience than I should have at that age. I had not yet become a refugee from the battles of sin in my life. I still thought I was having fun on the front lines. I was feeding my flesh with pornography, alcoholic beverages, and also dabbling in drugs. It was only marijuana at this stage, but unfortunately I thought it was hip for me to go to school "high." Maybe I had a misconception about what "high school" meant.

## On the Move

For reasons I cannot fully understand, we moved many times while I was growing up. God knows all the reasons we bounced back and forth between Northern Virginia and North Carolina. I now see how God used all of this to help prepare me for the mobile life of an overseas worker. I went to over seven different schools before reaching the 12th grade. When I started high school, we had just moved again. This time our journey led us from North Carolina back to Northern Virginia. My parents were on the verge of divorce, and my life was beginning to unravel. I was trying to adjust to the differences between my tiny K-12th grade school back in Coats, North Carolina, and my new school in Virginia. My freshman class at Stafford High School alone had more students than my former entire school district.

I was well on my way to a personal train wreck in high school. My older brother and his friends were supplying me with adult beverages and substances. Other dangerous items were also easily accessible in our house. I was growing up too fast, and the tempting trash around me was infecting my life. I was being drawn away by my own lust, as the Word of God describes in the Book of James. Indeed, the heart is exceedingly wicked as the Prophet Jeremiah proclaimed thousands of years ago. Feeding the flesh some form of filth was just as common as chewing my favorite peanut-butter-and-jelly sandwiches. Surprisingly, my schoolwork hadn't suffered much from my extracurricular activities. As one of the new students in school, I also had not had time to create a reputation. I thought of myself as an adventurous and independent spirit who still had life under control.

## Mercy Me!

Then, someone my own age offered me a gift of mercy. God brought Tyler into my life via my AP Biology class. We were both teenagers, talking the same mother tongue in the 9th grade. He was the first friend I had who did not pull me into things that messed up my life even more. Instead, I began to realize that Tyler had some qualities in his life that I did not have. I saw a sense of peace, hope, and real life in him—a different approach from the way I was living. As guys, naturally, these were not things we talked about. I don't know if I could have asked him. I was still trying to do things my way. I lived with the macho mentality of "Big boys don't cry" or "Only the weak ask for help."

Without a doubt, Tyler was a "flame" and I was the "front line." In September 1984, he invited me to a Billy Graham Evangelistic Association meeting that was held in the gym at our school. My mother and I went together. Something was going down that was beyond deductive reasoning. Ralph Bell, one of Graham's team, spoke. He gave a simple, direct message explaining the meaning of these words of the Messiah, "For God loved the world so much that He gave His one and only Son, so that everyone who believes in Him will not perish but have everlasting life" (John 3:16).

I had never heard anything like that before. I had no memory of being in a church service before that night, with the exception of weddings, and those recollections were clouded by the drunkenness and fights that seemed to always occur. I was told I did attend a Vacation Bible School at a church in Northern Virginia when I was very young, but got kicked out for putting gum in a little girl's hair—probably because she was cute and I liked her!

Listening in amazement to Ralph Bell that night, I could hardly believe my ears. What he was saying about God seemed too good to be true. He had my attention. I would not have called myself an atheist at that time. I knew there was a God, but I was ignoring Him. My family would have all said that there was a time and place for religion, but we never seemed to find the time or be in that place. When Ralph Bell started talking about God, I was at least willing to listen. The truth about forgiveness and reconciliation represented uncharted territory. I was hearing the wonderful Good News about Almighty God as a Loving Heavenly Father.

**Wooing Love**

Ralph explained that God's giving His only Son did not just mean that the Messiah came from heaven to earth. He described how Christ was miraculously conceived in flesh and blood...the mysterious incarnation of the Eternal Word of God becoming a man. He spoke of Christ's sinless life characterized by compassion and the miraculous. He went on to tell us that Jesus, the Savior of the world, died on the Cross to take away our sins and then rose from the dead to destroy the power of sin and death. I knew all about this power of sin and death; it had more influence in my life than I realized. I thought I would love to know this Person who can deliver me from the fear of death and the power of sin.

Ralph Bell made it clear that believing in the Lord Jesus meant more than simply admitting He existed or memorizing a creed. It was even more than reciting some ancient script like the Pledge of Allegiance we proudly and publically said in grade school. Don't get me wrong, I still cry sometimes at the reading of "The Apostle's Creed," however, salvation is from the Lord and it is an issue of the heart. He elaborated on the meaning of this miracle by saying saving faith involves putting all of one's faith in Christ alone and trusting Him with his or her entire life — past, present, and future.

He pleaded with us to transfer our full allegiance to the Lord Jesus Christ. He told us that our own righteousness or religion was not good enough to get us into heaven. He said, "God has provided the way, which is the free gift of eternal life through our Lord Jesus Christ, the Messiah." I felt that night as if I were getting an offer that was too good to refuse! A door seemed to open, and I couldn't think of a single reason why I should not walk through it. I didn't know what was on the other side, but I wanted to find out.

Just before he ended his sermon, Ralph invited anyone who was ready to accept God's free gift of salvation and follow the Lord Jesus to come and join him at the front for prayer. He reminded us that the Word of God declares that if we believe in our hearts that Jesus died for us and rose again from the dead to deliver us, and if we confess with our mouths that *Jesus is Lord*, we are saved, forgiven, put in a right relationship with God our Father. He told us the Bible says, "Whoever calls on the name of the Lord will be saved" and "By grace we are saved through faith, it is a gift of God, not of works so that no one can boast."

As the invitation started, I heard such a sweet sound as hundreds of voices sang, "Just as I am without one plea, but that Thy blood was shed for me and that Thou bid me come to Thee, Oh Lamb of God, I come." My heart was moved. I went forward to receive Jesus Christ as my Savior. We were led in a prayer admitting our own sinfulness and accepting God's free gift of salvation. I honestly did not understand everything that was going on, but I thought, "Why would I not want to turn my life over to God, knowing He would love and welcome me?" I prayed the prayer. It wasn't hard. Who would not want to do this? I knew I was a sinner. I needed forgiveness. I could not pass up this opportunity. My mother also went forward that night, though we never spoke much about the experience.

I vaguely recall someone visited us to follow up with further spiritual guidance a few days later. That memory includes a tinge of shame, because the person who came attended a church whose parking lot I had visited several years earlier to vandalize car tires. This served as a painful reminder of the wicked road I was traveling. Since we would soon relocate there was no opportunity to sink down any spiritual roots. Thus, with no church background and little support, the experience I had at the crusade remained a stone of remembrance with few direct results in my life. The first seeds, however, were planted. It was a grand opening of what would one day be a glorious garden.

## Dark Clouds Coming

Events soon transpired that made the next year confusing and perhaps the hardest of my life. My parents divorced. My resentment toward my father ran deep. I felt abandoned and betrayed. I suddenly found myself, with mixed emotions, as "the man of the house." By now, my parents had added two little sisters to the family, one still in diapers. My heart ached for my mother. I felt overwhelmed by the thought of her having to raise my little sisters on her own. I continually found myself angry with my father for what he had done and for the conflict his visits caused. Sometimes we had real fistfights. I have to admit that sometimes, in my rage, I wanted to kill my father for hurting us all.

I was determined not to let my mother down, but to help her in every way I could. My oldest brother, Phil, was already married, had his own family responsibilities and lived in another state. Jerry, my other older brother, was leaving for the Air Force. I was on the spot and a part of me instinctively rose to the challenge. Yes, the loss of my earthly father was excruciating. But, again, our Merciful Heavenly Father used it to further train me to serve my family and the needy people of Afghanistan. Painful episodes in life can produce greater purpose, if we allow the Hand of Providence to be the wise potter and us the willing clay.

During all this chaos, with the school year only half over, we moved back to Coats, North Carolina. Our frequent family moves were a mixture of divine steering and desperate survival. I began to make new friends, some of whom were regular churchgoers. I joined them at the Coats Baptist Church. It was fun to have the same group of friends at school, on the ball field, at the local arcade and in the church pew. The messages and teaching I heard began to fill the gaps in my understanding of the Bible and God's plan. Sundays were great. Youth group was fun. What a sweet, peaceful atmosphere. I knew what I was hearing was the truth and I loved it, but I lived in a different world during the week.

From Monday through Saturday I was wrestling with the teenage thing of puberty and peer pressure. I was still a mess. I felt bound by my family problems and youthful lusts, and even more paralyzed by my own past. The life I heard about on Sunday was the life I wanted. My heart was like a garden being sown with good seeds, but still infested with weeds. I was living the parable of the sower and the various types of soils that Jesus talked about to illustrate the Kingdom of God. As He explained it, I was in danger of being a garden whose seeds were snatched by the enemy or choked by the cares and temptations of the world.

I especially remember the challenges of starting high school, as well as the positive influence of the

Youth Pastor at Coats Baptist Church. His name was Keith Hall. He cared for us youngsters and worked hard to share Christ with us. He was a good gardener of the seeds in our hearts; however, it is not easy to work with troubled youth. I, like many others, was still stuck in the vicious cycle of teenage confusion. I could not find the way to overcome my own personal struggles. I just could not see the light at the end of the tunnel. Pastor Keith, however, did not fail to reach me in his labor of love. He was one of the many, like a link in the chain, whom the Sovereign One strategically used in my life. Some plant, some water, but God causes the seeds to grow.

**Triton High School**

During my sophomore year of high school, Harnett County's three small school districts, Dunn, Coats and Erwin, consolidated into one new building in Erwin, North Carolina. My world was developing. By now, I had my own lawn-mowing business, a part-time position at a grocery store and a janitor's job at the local clothing plant that my Grandmother Weaver supervised. I had my driver's license and my fancy Volkswagen Beetle Bug, which did not have a proper reverse gear. This forced me to leave early for school every morning to get the parking spot without a concrete slab, so I could pull the car in face first.

At Triton High, I also played tennis and ran cross-country. I was even inducted into the Beta Club, and my acting skills landed me an elected position in the Drama Club. I wasn't voted the most popular, but for many reasons everyone knew the Weavers from

Coats. I was now in the company of a larger circle of peers. This was both good and bad. Looking back, I see that, indeed, God had a divine plan.

# Chapter 4

# Reality Check

Among these potential new friends at my new high school, one beautiful red-headed girl caught my eye. Guess what? I fell in love. Well, maybe it was mixed with a bit of lust, which just caused me to fall even more. I soon discovered that she was from a whole family of churchgoers. To see her, I would have to attend her church, Fellowship Free Will Baptist Church in Dunn, North Carolina. It seemed a small sacrifice compared to what my heart was feeling. The church had a young fireball pastor, "a flame on the front line." He was a down-to-earth guy, yet a great communicator of heavenly truth. I remember thinking, "Wow, this is pretty cool."

It was a new church, but still the same struggle for me. I listened to the passionate messages about the Cross of Christ and found myself thinking, "Yeah, I believe this! I agree with you. I really want to experience what you are talking about—I want to live this way!" Looming like a mountain range, however, were all my problems: past sins, pride, anger and lust. I was living a double life, straddling the fence between the Sunday sermon and sinful sensuality. I still followed the ways of the world more than the Word of God. My earthly passions were still burning brighter than the eternal flame that would soon over-come them.

## Somebody Is Praying

Later I discovered that the young pastor, Mike Trimble, and his wife, Terry, had been truly praying for us. They not only interceded for my family and me, but also specifically pleaded for all the young people of church, backed up by expressions of tender care for us. They knew enough about our lives to beseech the Lord to help us get right with Him. That was certainly my case as the wayward sheep.

They even asked that some of us become apos-tles, prophets, evangelists, pastors and, teachers. They interceded faithfully, believing there were future missionaries in their midst. They persevered, trusting that Lord of Harvest still calls many young people into His fields that are white for harvest. Every day they lifted us to the throne of grace, requesting that we be set free from selfishness and sent out to serve in His Vineyard. Others in the church were also praying that we become passionate followers of the Lord Jesus. Surely the parents of my high school sweetheart were regularly on their knees. I believe those prayers not only protected me but also protected others from me. But would the prayers of the saints bear fruit? Would I ever become a flame burning brightly for the world to see?

My first few years attending that church passed with few noticeable changes in my life. Sunday after Sunday I was taking in what was good, but I wasn't giving out much in return. I was being blessed, but I wasn't doing much blessing. Perhaps the positive influence of the Fellowship Free Will Baptist Church helped more than I realized, because I did graduate from Triton High School. Now the hot and humid North Carolina summer had passed, I was 18 years old and a freshman in college.

## A Breakthrough

Without an understanding God's sovereignty, I chose to attend Campbell University, a school close to home. I still saw myself as the savior of my mother and sisters. My mother had become a single parent trying to juggle long work hours with the demands of two little girls at home. I could not leave them. The young lady who had been my original reason for attending the church was now out of the picture. She and most of my graduating class had left the area for distant schools. Some of the distractions of my life, therefore, had gradually been replaced by responsibilities. A divine deal was developing. God was indeed up to something.

Campbell University was very convenient because it was only a five-minute drive from our house. The Hand of Providence, however, was interested in more than my saving a few dollars on the fuel bill. I didn't think much about Campbell having a Baptist heritage. Soon, however, in my very first semester of college, I found myself sitting in a religious studies class. The course didn't offer much direction, other than the realization that many people my age were also struggling with ultimate life issues. One day we had a discussion over, "Who is Jesus Christ the Messiah?" that left me with more questions than answers. Yet something in my conscience was pricked that day and my consciousness was curiously peaked.

Then something started burning in my heart. Without obvious warnings or conscious choices on my part, the seeds of truth that had been planted and watered in my heart began to germinate and grow. An increase was coming. The reaping-and-sowing principle of the kingdom proved true. I could sense the glow of God's presence breaking through the haze of my life like the sun warming a garden after a cloudy morning.

I phoned Pastor Mike to respond to an announcement he made the week before. There was going to be a conference at First Free Will Baptist Church in Raleigh, North Carolina. Pastor Mike had extended an invitation to anyone who might be interested in attending with him. I eagerly wanted to go, but I had no clue what to expect. It was Tuesday, November 15, 1988. I made plans to get off work for the evening.

Pastor Mike and I made the trip together. He did not know how much had been going on in my heart, nor did I understand it well enough to explain it to him. I only knew God had been speaking to me and drawing me to Himself by His love. Even as

God was overwhelming me with His goodness and mercy, I was also becoming more and more aware of my selfish sinfulness and my need to make serious changes in my life. God's kindness was about to carry me to the door marked "Repentance," which, if entered, would lead to the joyous victory that comes through surrender.

That night, an American who had been serving the Lord in Uruguay was the featured speaker. He told stories about the way God was transforming the lives of people in Uruguay and how the church was growing there. The thrust of his message was, "Study this Book of Instruction continually. Meditate on it day and night so you will be sure to obey everything written in it. Only then will you prosper and succeed in all you do. This is my command—be strong and courageous! Do not be afraid or discouraged. For the LORD your God is with you wherever you go." (Joshua 1:8-9).

He emphasized two unforgettable points in his message. The first had to do with the encouragement God's children can find in the first verses of Joshua about strength and success. Those who fully surrender to the Lord have the promise of divine power and provisions. He went on to trace Joshua's career of service and closed the message with the challenge of Joshua 24:15, "Choose this day whom you will serve.....But as for me and my house, we will serve the Lord." The Word of God spoke right into my heart: *John, choose who you are going to serve!*

## Face Down

There were hundreds of people in the crowd, but I knew this message was for me. I thought about the past several years of my life and the continuous responses that I had been making each time I heard God's Word: "Yeah, that's cool. I believe it. I understand what you're saying. I would truly love to experience it." On this particular night, things came to a head. The Word of God was like a double-edged sword in my heart.

I felt compelled to respond in spite of the questions I still had. The Holy Spirit was convicting me of sin, but at the same time revealing the redeeming love of the Father. The prophet Jeremiah spoke of how God draws us to Himself with cords of kindness. His mercy met me in a way that I wanted to be close to Him. I longed to experience Him and to give myself completely to Him. A tide surged in me that I can only describe as a desire for God. It was as if a flame began burning in my soul.

When the altar call was given, I responded and went forward to the front of the church. It was a typical invitation at the close of the service, but this time it was more than a routine thing for me. The compelling voice of the Lord was clear. God's gentle touch broke me. His tender hand humbled me. Crying my eyes out, I bowed face down in deep contrition and absolute surrender to the King of all creation. What else could I do in that moment of encountering the Divine One and His holy love?

I found myself weeping and pouring out my heart: "Lord, I do believe in You. You are the Way;

You are the Answer. I do trust in You, for You died and rose again. You are my only hope and I surrender to You. Have mercy on me. Have Your way with me. Here's my heart, my life, take all of me. I do want to serve You. Thank You for loving me, saving me and choosing me to be Your child. Thank You for calling me out of darkness into Your kingdom of light. Thank You, Heavenly Father, Thank You!"

## Chains Broke

This intense experience included significant amounts of repentance and renewal. The teacher in me wants to explain exactly where that evening fits in the sequence of God's work in my life, but I hesitate to do so. It was definitely a life-changing, spiritual turning point. My chains were gone, my conscience was cleansed and I rose from the prostrate position transformed by the presence of God. It was an encounter with my Heavenly Father in a way I had never experienced—almost as if His Spirit set me ablaze.

The lights were now on, and things started making sense. Seeds! It was about God planting the eternal kernel of His Word in my heart and then bringing forth the increase. I remembered my first encounter with God back at the crusade four years ago, which was an undeniable starting point. Without that beginning, I do not know what would have brought me to Raleigh, the place the Sovereign One ordained for me that night.

I continually discover that there were specific moments in my life when God broke through in ways that had some kind of significant effect on me. For example, often I heard my mother speak the memorized words of a hopeful prayer by Robert Schuler as she drove her happy hoodlums to school in the morning.

And who could forget our great aunt, Rena? I wanted to know what was special about the little widow, but I never asked. At our big family reunions, although the smallest among us, she stood out like a shining star. In the presence of those who were ungrateful, irreligious or vulgar, she was a "flame on the front line." Her character of love, peace, thankfulness and selfless service was not only noticeable, but also attractive. She made a powerful impact and lasting impression on me. Later, I learned that she knew the Lord Jesus long before I met Him. And she prayed faithfully for the salvation of many of us in her extended family. We shared a special bond and sweet times of fellowship until she went to be with the Lord.

## Free at Last

Whatever terms you use to define what happened to me that night in Raleigh, the results were dramatic. However you slice it the analysis is the same. It was a *reality check*. I suddenly had a hunger to read and understand the Bible for myself. I wanted to pray and did so for hours. I desired to find and follow God's will for my life. I sensed an immediate freedom to speak to others about my own experience of God's love and forgiveness. I discovered an amazing change in the way I thought about the past. When I surrendered my life to the Lord that night, it was as if I had turned over ownership of everything connected with my life, including the ugly baggage of sin and the struggles that I had faced alone. The load was lifted. I was forgiven! No more burden or guilt—I was free!

To my surprise, I no longer felt the same way about my dad, even though I hadn't had the chance to tell him yet. That time would come later. I found myself reacting to situations and responding to people differently. My way of thinking improved, like an attitude adjustment or a new computer chip in the software or hardware of my mind. I knew I was not perfect, but I could not deny that I had changed.

The Bible says: "And so, dear brothers and sisters, I plead with you to give your bodies to God because of all He has done for you. Let them be a living and holy sacrifice—the kind He will find acceptable. This is truly the way to worship Him. Don't copy the behavior and customs of this world, but let God transform you into a new person by changing the way you think. Then you will learn to know God's will for you, which is good and pleasing and perfect." (Romans 12:1–2).

In view of God's mercy, we are to present ourselves as living sacrifices and the effects are wonderful: a way out of conformity with the world, a renewing of the mind, and a sense of God's will for our lives. These were all major struggles that had plagued me before this point of surrender. Wow, what a spiritual overhaul! I was joining a power greater than myself on an adventurous, unforgettable journey. You might call it a voyage with eternity in view, a highway to holiness or a road of righteousness on the pathway of peace. All the passions that previously pursued fleshly frivolity were now like funnels tapped into God's fountain of pure delight. God was consuming me with His own fire that now had me inflamed with a burning passion for Him.

# Chapter 5

# Step by Step

My friends in Afghanistan love to speak in proverbs. Some serve as great illustrations for this section of the book, for example, "Drop by drop a river is formed." One invaluable lesson I'm still learning while working in Afghanistan is said this way, "Arriving late is better than not arriving at all." I forgot to mention all our family car accidents. We would have greatly benefited from adopting this Afghan proverb. It is frequently quoted on long road trips in the mountains of Afghanistan. It is designed to serve a dual purpose of encouraging endurance and securing safety. One of our remote road systems stretches over a 4,000-meter pass, so the word on the street is "Be careful." Because it is such a steep, dirt road and the vehicle only moves a few miles per hour, the word is "I think we can, I think we can."

Afghans seem to have the long view in sight. They often speak about "going slowly" or "There is a path to the top of even the highest mountain." I marvel at how the Hand of Providence gently guided me step by step and prepared me for every bend in the road. I wasn't always quick to learn the lessons in the ebb and flow of life, but God was patiently teaching me with the principles expressed so well by my Afghan friends. I do see our Heavenly Father's faithful provision and how in every season there were preparations for the next. One of my favorite songs by Rich Mullins says, "Oh, God, You are my God and I will ever praise You, and I will seek You in the morning and learn to walk in Your ways, and step by step You lead me and I will follow You all of my days." God has used this song many times to encourage me to press on.

Meanwhile, back home in Coats, I began to think about the next step. My heart said, "I want to go somewhere to just study the Bible. I don't have a biblical background. My life is void of a spiritual heritage or scriptural foundation. I want to carefully and diligently build one." It was still November 1988. I met several times with Pastor Mike, discussing options for the future as my first semester at Campbell University was coming to an end. I had already visited and considered several possible schools.

One road trip stands out. I traveled with several other North Carolinian youths to Nashville, Tennessee, to check out Free Will Baptist Bible College (FWBBC). It turned out to be a nonstop, action-packed weekend, which included a full campus tour, a basketball game, special speakers, cookouts and chapel services. The extrovert in me loved it, but it was too noisy and busy to think or pray. The ride back to Coats was filled with laughter and stories, but I could hardly wait to be alone and seek the face of God. It was time to be still and listen for the still small voice. My car was at the church in Smithfield, North Carolina, where we were dropped off. I had an hour's drive home to sort things out. I kept praying, "Lord, what's happening here? What should I do next? Father, Your will be done! Please speak to me."

I tried to evaluate my situation. My semester at Campbell had just ended. There were plenty of reasons for staying in Coats, North Carolina. I had a scholarship from Campbell, so tuition wasn't very expensive. I could stay at home and be the "head of the house"—and maybe I needed to for the sake of my mother and sisters. Yet I wanted to go some place where I could seriously study the Bible. I didn't matter where, as long as the school would immerse me in God's Word. By the time I got home, I sensed that God was directing me to attend FWBBC in Nashville, Tennessee. The words of a Michael W. Smith song echoed in my ears, "Go west young man." But what about my responsibilities at home? God was saying, "John, I will take care of your mom and sisters. After all, I am God, the Heavenly Father. You just trust and obey."

### Real Reason

I immediately took steps to put my life in order. I got an extra job over the holidays to earn money for room and board at school. I applied to Free Will

Baptist Bible College, contacted personal references, and filled out numerous forms to prepare for the change. My new school had a dress code that required an upgraded wardrobe with ties and sport coats—I had to get cleaned up! I told pastor Mike and the brothers and sisters at Fellowship Church that God was directing me to study in Nashville. Some were even more excited than I was about this good news.

This transformation process began to affect my whole life. I never disagreed with the phrase, "Jesus is the reason for the season," but this Christmas was different for I sincerely desired to celebrate the reality of the Christ-child. This involved new steps in the right direction. I began reading the Scriptures regularly and studying the hundreds of prophecies about the Messiah. God moved me to give my family and friends gifts that plant seeds of love and encouragement. I distinctly remember one particular book, *God Calling*, which I gave to my great aunt, Anne. She was an elderly widow who lived alone. God often reminded me to pray for her. He used this book to bring her to salvation, which was so sweet to witness. What an honor to co-labor with the Sovereign Creator and Savior of all. I also attended several worship services over the holiday season. I even went to church on New Years Eve and welcomed 1989 with prayers for God's favor and the salvation of my family.

One Sunday morning, early in January, I was asked to speak to the congregation and share how God had worked in my life. Pastor Mike assured me that the brothers and sisters would want to know my story so that they could pray and support me. That

Sunday my entire family showed up for the service. God was already answering my prayers. Friends from high school days also came. They knew my history and wanted to know what really happened to me! I told them as clearly as I could what God had done and where He was leading me. Though many of them, including some of my family, did not fully understand the changes, I considered their support and encouragement that day priceless. It was a comfort knowing many others were with me as I set off on my journey to Nashville.

It's interesting to think about some pieces of this puzzle that God had shaped beforehand. A few months earlier, at my mother's insistence, we had managed to scrape together a down payment to buy a new Mitsubishi Precis. Unknown to me, it was prophetic. Who would have thought that five months later I would be driving off to college almost 600 miles away? As thankful as my mother had been for my willingness to stay around, she also blessed my departure in the little blue car. It wasn't easy—heart wrenching, to say the least. Perhaps she understood even better than I did how much I needed to go where God was leading me.

## A Tribute to Mom

My hat is off to my mom, Sandra Virginia Hoover. She was born and raised in Northern Virginia, the youngest of three children. Her first love resulted in an unplanned pregnancy when she was 16 years old. She delivered her first-born son, my oldest brother Phil. Motherly responsibilities prevented my mom from finishing high school and, sadly, things did not work out with her high-school sweetheart. Shortly thereafter, a handsome young man in the Navy married my mom and "adopted" her son. My mom and dad experienced their first sorrow when their first baby, a girl, lived only a few minutes after birth. Later that year, their first-born son entered the world and they named him Jerry, Jr. I was not in the picture yet, and the two beautiful daughters would come years later.

My family moved almost every year. Experiences like this can make you stronger, but they can also wear you out. Multiple moves are especially hard on mothers, who were designed to help nurture their families and make the house a home. Our place of residence was not only in constant change; we boys kept it quite lively. Raising three sons, with an over-worked husband and then two daughters, is not easy for even the most qualified mothers. Perhaps there were times when my mom wondered if she was losing it. Our numerous and various stages of rebellion, the worry we caused, the friends we associated with, the trouble we got into, and the hell we raised was enough to drive her crazy.

The saddest part of my mom's story was the unraveling of her relationship with my dad. Regardless of "why or why not," my mom faced the hardest blow when her marriage ended. In most cases death is easier than divorce. Divorce has no real conclusion. It is something God never intended.

God does not like divorce. He spoke clearly through the prophet Malachi, "Didn't the LORD make you one with your wife? And what does He want? Godly children from your union. So guard your heart; remain loyal to the wife of your youth 'For I hate divorce! To divorce your wife is to overwhelm her with cruelty. So guard your heart; do not be unfaithful to your wife.' says the LORD of Heaven's Armies, the God of Israel." (Malachi 2:15-16).

In the words of the Messiah, "From the beginning God made them male and female. This explains why a man leaves his father and mother and is joined to his wife, and the two are united into one. Since they are no longer two but one, let no one split apart what God has joined together." (Matthew 19). This is why our marriage vows read till death do us part.

If I could have one wish this Christmas, it would be a cure for divorce. Inside America over half of all marriages end in divorce, and therefore, thousands upon thousands of boys and girls suffer in some way because of it. Many moms and dads feel the pain, too. As a parent I must realize that if I am too absent from the home, because of work or other legitimate reasons, it will affect my children. If I break my marriage vows, however, it will drastically affect the psyche of those I helped bring into the world.

The power of a parent's presence was clearly illustrated when Paris, the daughter of the late Michael Jackson, squeezed the microphone and talked about her wonderful daddy and how much she loved him. My eyes filled with tears as I heard her and again now as I try to write this. If you heard her sweet voice, you were probably teary-eyed too, and in 50 years we might well remember her tender words more than those of "Thriller." Such is the importance of a daddy, a mommy. A husband-wife parenting team is even more powerful.

As difficult as death is, there is closure. The Bible helps us by describing death. Our earthly destiny is death, where we breathe no more. Human experience also prepares us. No one has lived forever. I remember when my mom lost her Aunt Martha, the twin sister of her own mother. It was heartbreaking as we saw cancer literally eat the flesh off her bones. The sting of death is awful. But there is finality. She "passed away," as we say in English. Now on earth all we have left are precious memories of her.

My mom's next tragedy was the death of her father, Ralph Warren Hoover. Several soldiers saluted the veteran and father of three on August 13, 1996, at Arlington National Cemetery. Just prior to his departure he could remember when his third child, Sandra Virginia, was still a twinkle in his eye. My grandfather had his own traumatic experience in World War II. After seeing so much destruction and death during the war, I imagine he was glad to be a part of the intimate life-giving process. Shortly after returning from military service overseas, by the mercy of God, he fathered his last child. "Little Sandy" brought joy to her happy and proud daddy, and was blessed to have parents who stayed together through the heavens and hells of life.

My mom's parents remained married for nearly 60 years, which is interesting writing this from Afghanistan where the life expectancy is under 50. While my grandparents' relationship wasn't perfect, seeing them committed "till death do us part" had impact on us all. Now mom faced the agony of letting go of her earthly father, on top of her own family struggles. It wasn't easy...and who would take care of her mother, a widow living alone in an apartment in Northern Virginia? My mom was now residing back in North Carolina, because it was the birthplace of my dad and where our last family move took us.

My mom's mother, Mary Catherine Malone, would live eight more years after saying goodbye to her lifelong husband. Seeing her was always a highlight of my return trips from Afghanistan. Sometimes I would fly into Washington, D.C., take a taxi to her apartment and surprise her with flowers. The journey was planned, and my mom was on her way, driving up I-95 to meet us. We just didn't always tell my grandmother. These surprises spiced up our lives. We also had sweet fellowship from time to time reading the Bible and praying together. It was a bittersweet experience when she went to be with the Lord, heartbreaking for my mom, who was with her that morning at her apartment in Northern Virginia.

The family gave me the honor of sharing God's Word at Granny Hoover's funeral, which I did with tears in my eyes. She is now beside my grandfather at Arlington National Cemetery. But only her human remains are there. Her eternal soul or spirit is in Heaven with the Father. She is in Beulah Land, the place of no more pain or sorrow. For the Bible tells us, if we are absent from the body then we are present with the Lord. This is the living hope or assurance of the children of God. Unlike the hopelessness among many of my Afghan friends, because of Jesus, the Resurrection and the Life, we can say, "O death, where is your victory? O death, where is your sting? For sin is the sting that results in death, and the law gives sin its power. But thank God! He gives us victory over sin and death through our Lord Jesus Christ." (I Corinthians 15:55-57).

My Mom has experienced much over the years: divorce, deaths of both parents and close family members, frequent family moves, financial difficulties and the challenges of raising five children in modern America. Then, after investing so much parental energy, mostly as a single mom, she had to comfort herself five times as we left the house one by one. This, too, is a loss that needs preparation.

Mom is now alone with an empty nest. My eldest brother, Phil, married after high school and started his own family. Jerry left home for the Air Force, only to "shoot down his own plane" because of his drug addiction. I left for Nashville, Music City USA, not to hit the big time or make a record, but to study the Bible. Then, my next younger sister, Mary Martha, headed to college and later married a nice young man from Wilson, North Carolina. Last, but not least, Sandi Lynn, completely emptied the nest as she moved on to college to pursue a career as a financial analyst.

My mom had always lived with family around. Now it is just her and the outside cat, Boots, in our little house in Coats, North Carolina. Mom is miracle of survival, because there is another side to the story. She, far from sainthood, has a strong faith in the Lord

Jesus Christ. At times you find her singing, praying, reading the Bible—leaning on the Lord. Her life clearly communicates that we need God's healing grace to forgive and grieve our losses well. God is her Heavenly Father, the Lover of her soul and the Faithful One who promises never to leave or forsake her.

The complex Weaver family situation is not easy, even if Mom never says so, and any therapist would see the stress involved. Our story would fill a book. It has affected all of us in some way. The Bible says, "All have sinned and come short of the glory of God." Our dysfunction as a family compounded this downward trend to moral decay. Thankfully, that is not the end of the story. My mom is still working, enjoying life and seizing each day by finding opportunities to serve others in some way. We are all extremely grateful for the gracious gift God gave us wrapped up in our precious little blonde-haired mother, known to so many as "Sandy." Praise God for His amazing grace that found her.

In the intervening years there have been some healthy changes and happy additions to my family. My eldest brother, Phil, is the father of three beautiful daughters and has two grandchildren. My other older brother, Jerry, who was a drug addict, gives much of his time and energy to helping others find deliverance from addictions. He just celebrated 20 years of sobriety, hooray! Jerry is also successful in his work and happily married to a wonderful lady named Sarah. My sister, Mary, and her husband, Thomas, have a beautiful little girl and a bouncing boy. Mary serves the community as a social worker. Sweet Sandi Lynn is now married and has an adorable baby girl. I had the honor of pronouncing Jerry and Sarah, Thomas and Mary, and Erick and Sandi "husband and wife." Please don't think I forgot about my dad. God healed our hearts and reconciled our relationship. I love my dad very much, and he is proud of his son, John Mack Weaver III.

## Off to Music City

Let us return to the story. In January 1989, I said good-bye to North Carolina and hello to Nashville, Tennessee. I transferred from Campbell University to Free Will Baptist Bible College. The hardest step was leaving my mom and saying "Farewell for now" to my younger sisters. Our Afghan friends often say, *"Tawakul ba Khudo,"* which means "Given over to God." It is the idea that "It belongs to God" or "It is in His Hands." I knew the best place for all of us was in God's Hands. Nonetheless, moving on was a painful experience. I sobbed the first hours of my voyage alone on I-40 from Raleigh to Nashville.

As I set out on the westward voyage, this new-found passion for what God wanted to build into my life was like a flame burning in my heart. I was filled with awe, excitement and anticipation. Yet I still hadn't given much thought to what God might have for me in calling or vocation. It didn't really matter because soon I began to discover the wealth of His Word and a world of service in which He allowed me to play a part. What an awesome God!

# Chapter 6

# Found: FWBBC

I have been amazed during my time in Afghani-stan how something from my past prepared me for the places where God allowed me to serve. I am convinced that God our Heavenly Father does not waste any experience. We're always in training. He can even use our mistakes to mature us. Difficulty is designed to develop stamina in us. Hardships can humble us and help prepare us to handle future assignments. I didn't particularly enjoy moving as much as we did when I was growing up, but the frequent relocations forced me to learn a lot about making friends and adapting to new circumstances. God was using these situations to train me long before I was ready to participate in His global work on the planet.

Speaking of preparation, I am so grateful for the five years I spent studying at Free Will Baptist Bible College. I arrived at FWBBC in January 1989. Other than some casual acquaintances from the Welcome

Weekend I had attended in December, I knew no one on campus, but was confident that the Good Shepherd led me to the dormitory called Goen Hall. God began to add details to His basic guidance.

For starters, my courses required that I spend hours studying God's Word on my own. It was a daily discovery: from Old Testament Survey, Biblical Doctrines, Systematic Theology, to New Testament Survey. The voyage only got better and as we went deeper into the Gospels, the Epistles, the Pastoral Letters and the Prophetic Books. Day after day the Word of God was transforming my mind. Day after day God gave me more and more nuggets of truth. I was like a sponge soaking it all in.

My favorite class focused on the book of Ephesians. My professor, Dr. Woodard, encouraged me to memorize the book. It was a delightful, transforming experience. I also remember encountering the writings of those who have gone before us, like Saint Augustine, Martin Luther, John Calvin, Charles and John Wesley, and Jonathan Edwards. What an impact that had on me, along with books by A. W. Tozer, Andrew Murray, Charles Spurgeon, Oswald Chambers, and Billy Graham. My spiritual famine began to get generous doses of relief. What a delight to my thirsty soul.

As an extreme extrovert, I quickly got to know other people. It is also one of the unique characteristics of the school. Year after year, ever since the school started in 1942, God has always formed lasting relationships among the students. I specifically remember two older students who took me under their wings. God used them greatly in my life, and as the Bible says, "Iron sharpens iron." In many ways, Tim and Jamie mentored me and daily "discipled" me—offering me friendship, role models as Christian men, and practical counsel based on their longer experience following Jesus. One became a very close companion, like a Jonathan-and-David kind of relationship. Jamie and I are still good friends today.

## In the House

I distinctly remember one of our first conversations at college. "Jamie, where do you go to church?" I asked. I could tell by his hesitancy that he did not want to answer. "John, you don't want to go with me. You need to find a good church," he replied. "What do you mean?" I asked. "If you want me to go to a good church, then just what kind of church are you going to?"

It turned out he was involved in a tiny congregation called Friendship Church. It was a Christian service ministry in an area of Nashville where many pimps and prostitutes lived. At the time there were only about 10 people attending the little house church. How interesting that *my first church* experience while studying at FWBBC was in a *house*. Maybe you haven't heard, but there are no official churches in Afghanistan. The population is approaching 30 million and there are more than 40,000 Islamic mosques, but there are still no public places for Christian worship. Those who follow the Messiah meet together in the privacy of their own homes. Some who serve among Afghans have the vision of a "lighthouse" movement.

Back at FWBBC I was thinking: "This house church and area interests me. Why not go and help Jamie and the people at Friendship Church? What a unique opportunity to serve the poor and share the wonderful love of Jesus Christ that is changing my life. Why not go where I am needed the most?" I did join Jamie. I started helping with the children, teaching them the stories of the Bible. This Christian service was pure enjoyment. I loved it! I remember the first time Jamie asked me if I would preach for him. He needed a substitute while he was out of town. I told him, "Yeah, that sounds awesome; I'll do it!" but inside I was scared to death. My mind said, "You are only 19 years old, you can't preach." God did give me something to say. I wrote out my first sermon, and it was 12 pages long.

That Sunday morning we gathered as usual. There were about a dozen of us. I led the whole worship service, including the singing. That was the first miracle, because I cannot sing. We worshipped and prayed, and I got ready to share God's Word. I basically read my notes, all 12 pages. I really didn't know what else to do. This was all new for me. I had only been at college for a few months, and I was still learning how to find things in the Bible.

Well, revival did not break out. It was just a regular service. Afterward, I took a few people home and headed back to school. On the way I thought about that time of ministry. I asked God, "Father, how did I do?" About the time those words left my lips a car passed by with the following words on the license plate: **WELL DONE**. I began to weep and laugh. I normally don't seek signs like this. But this was too obvious to overlook. For me it definitely was a clear word from the Lord that He was pleased with His child. It was another sovereign reminder to me that I was exactly where He wanted me to be.

## Brother Eddie

One of my professors, Eddie Payne, had recently arrived from many years of ministry in Côte d'Ivoire, West Africa. He had returned to the United States to head up the Intercultural Studies program at the college. He, along with Dr. Miley, a medical doctor who had also served in Africa, became my living introduction to a healthy perspective on world outreach. Brother Eddie became a close friend and mentor. He introduced me to the great biographies of people like William Carey, Samuel Zwemer, David Livingstone and Hudson Taylor. He also encouraged me to read the stories of George Mueller, Charles Finney, D. L. Moody, Corrie ten Boom, and Keith Green. These devoted lives were used by God to shape my thinking and to fuel a passion to serve Him. They were all "flames on the front line" in their own generation.

During my studies, I participated in various student conferences. One is well known by the name Urbana. Every few years some 20,000 university students gather to sing the praises of God, study His word and see how better to serve the needs of peoples of the Planet Earth. I traveled alone to Illinois to attend this one. I enjoyed every minute of it, like a little boy in a candy shop. Even though I went by myself, that was God's sovereign plan, for He was up to something. The conference speakers, seminars and songs sung by thousands were enough to bless my socks off.

## Spotlight

Our Heavenly Father, however, wanted to work deeper in my heart. Remember, I went alone. I was out of my comfort zone and the familiarity of FWBBC. God in His wisdom and love strategically placed me in a position of extreme vulnerability. It culminated in an experience that is hard to describe. At one meeting, a much respected Christian leader shared very openly about healing broken relationships. He used his interaction with his earthly father as the platform to address the subject. His presentation was a journey from brokenness to wholeness. After the picture was clearly painted, there was a long pause. Then a team of intercessors came to minister to those among us who needed relational healing. After the time of silence, one of them approached the microphone and said a simple prayer, "Come Holy Spirit." This faith-filled invitation, which no doubt was bathed in much united prayer, produced the most miraculous results.

The holy hush continued. Soon, spontaneous crying could be heard in various places of the large auditorium. By now, my eyes were shedding tears, even though I didn't know why. I wasn't sure what was happening. Suddenly, God exposed my heart and showed me some hidden rooms within that needed His cleansing and healing. The main one was my relationship with my dad. As I began to weep uncontrollably, God showed me a picture of myself in the pool at my grandmother's apartment where I often played with my little sister. Sometimes, while throwing a ball to each other, I would try to trick her by saying "look over there Sandy" and then put the ball between my legs under the water. Then, I would throw my hands up in the air and ask, "Where did the ball go?"

God in His mysterious way used this image to show me that I was still hiding something. Although I had forgiven my dad, deep in my heart there was still bottled up pain and anger toward him. On the outside I looked fine. Inwardly, however, I was wounded and pretending that the hidden hurt wasn't there like the ball I was hiding under the water, until, I was all alone at Urbana. God showed up. His spotlight penetrated past every obstacle and exposed the truth.

As God continued His loving work during this very personal experience, I saw myself in the pool letting go of the ball that was suppressed underwater. Every time I did this there was a release of force followed by the ball splashing out of the water. Somehow I understood what this meant. Now that the hidden things were in the light, I was simply to let go, take my hands off of them and experience a sense of release. The result was like a splash as the Spirit of God touched me afresh. I felt brand new, fully free to receive and give forgiveness. I wanted to run and catch the next plane to North Carolina and embrace my dad with the redeeming love of God our

Father. Well, the small town of Coats doesn't have an airport and, besides, God still had me in His operating room at Urbana.

## Korea

Another student gathering that profoundly impacted my life occurred in 1990. Our student prayer group was convinced that God wanted our whole campus to be a part of an event called the GO (Global Outreach) Conference in Georgia. It was a gathering for students considering how they might serve God in the world. It involved concerts of prayer, times of praise and worship, and seminars and discussion groups with older, more experienced servants of the Lord Jesus.

Our college only had about 300 students at the time. We began praying and asking specifically for financial scholarships and buses for transportation. By the time the GO Conference rolled around in November, we had more than 100 students ready to go. God inspired the faculty of the college to give enough money to subsidize the cost for each student. God also provided two coach buses to use on this road trip from Nashville to the conference site near Atlanta, Georgia. What an adventure we had!

Two personal memories stand out for me. I met my first Christian brother from Korea, Paul Aan. Wow, he was a flame brightly burning, who demonstrated a great passion for worship and prayer. Paul was really on fire for the Lord. In our prayer walks he challenged me to develop this passion in my own daily intimacy with God. One night after our corporate time of worship, in a moment of holy hush a speaker came on stage in full Arab dress. He spoke to us very forcefully from a Muslim perspective about the inconsistencies and hypocrisy that Christians so often show the world. He reminded us that Muslims do have valid complaints about Christians. "Frankly," he said, "you Christians are often lousy witnesses to the world about what you say you believe." His vivid message still echoes in my mind today!

**Fired-Up**

Since a third of our student body experienced this awesome conference, it created a new sense of urgency and commitment in the spiritual life on campus. Flickers were turning to flames. Daily life got a fresh jolt of God's Spirit at work in our lives. More of us gathered day by day to pray for laborers to be sent to all the unreached peoples. FWBBC was already structured in a way that gave priority to both academic excellence and practical service. Therefore, students were expected to be involved in outreach ministries and prayer groups.

What seemed to be structure or even a require-ment quickly turned into a passionate love for me, as I joined with others to serve and pray for our world. I took a course called "Perspectives" that gave me an eye-opening exposure to world events, human suffering, and entire ethnic cultures or "people groups" that have never been exposed to the Good News of Jesus Christ. This was another resourceful tool at that time and for the tremendous challenges that awaited me while serving overseas, especially in the Land of the Afghans.

**Wordless**

Speakers from various Christian agencies visited to share firsthand accounts of God's sovereign work in the world. Those involved in cross-cultural ministries seemed to connect with my awakening awareness that I might be of some use to God in the world. These groups emphasized language learning, cultural adaptation, linguistic analysis, community development, and sharing God's Word in relevant ways. Some of the guest speakers illustrated their talks with exciting stories about the principles of translation and the effects of God's Word in cultures whose languages have never been written down. It sounded thrilling.

There I was, a privileged student, falling in love with the Bible. In a sense I was experiencing the same wonderful discoveries these servants of God were reporting. I knew what it was like to be a "Bible-less person." I remembered what it was like to be lost in a sea of darkness. I understood the words of Prophet Amos, "there is a famine for hearing the Word of the Lord." Now, I found it a pleasure getting up in the morning to read God's Word, memorizing verses, spending time with fellow worshippers, and going into the community to share our faith. I could also relate to the changes that come when we are found by Christ, the Savior.

On one memorable occasion, a professional translator visited the school and did a "monolingual demonstration" with a Japanese student who was attending. This involves a presentation in which someone from one language group begins to learn the language of another group without the help of a translator. He used listening skills and phonetic techniques, along with pointing, mimicking, and showing objects or actions that provoked responses from the student that he would immediately write down. The process was hilarious, but the results caught my attention. Even a difficult language like Japanese could be learned if someone were willing to take on the challenge. I felt myself drawn and ready to sign up just for the experience.

The translator ended his presentation by asking us to quote John 3:16 with him. Talk about exposing my own spiritual roots. I could hardly utter those familiar phrases without choking up. I remembered how God had used those words to invite me to follow Him back in September 1984: "For God so loved the world," words that speak of pure love. This truth captured my heart. Then the speaker held up a huge blank poster and said, "Now, would you please read what's written here." After a moment of curious, dead silence as we stared at that empty surface, he said, "This is John 3:16 in about three thousand languages."

The silence that followed was different. It was so quiet even I could hear the Spirit whisper. The translator's statement stunned and broke me. I wept uncontrollably. I couldn't get over the hopelessness the empty poster represented. With tears rolling down my face I prayed, "Father, whatever You want me to be, I'll be, and whatever You want me to do, I'll do. If You can use me to do something about this, here am I, send me." It sounds almost amusing when I talk to people about a sense of calling; some ask me if I heard God speaking audibly or just felt drawn to serve in my spirit. I can honestly respond, "I didn't see any writing on the wall. What I saw was no writing at all where there should have been, and that was my call." In ways I am still discovering, God has given me the privilege to serve Him by filling in blank spaces in people's lives.

I remember that day as my first conscious surrender to a sense of call to spiritual service. Prior to that, others who had heard me speak about God's work in my life or teach the Scriptures had been telling me that I was called to be a preacher. I was grateful for their encouragement of abilities I was developing, but I was never comfortable with their conclusion. You have to consider that I was traveling in Christian circles where you answered the call to preach. That's basically what "calling" was all about—not that I don't thoroughly enjoy preaching. I can sermonize at the drop of a hat or with a moment's invitation. I had come to realize that those who can preach are not necessarily called to do so as a vocation. After all, Jesus told *all* of His disciples to go and preach the gospel (Mark 16:15). For Christians, the question it is not, "Will you share the gospel?" Rather, it is, *"How* will you share the gospel?"

All this was going on when I still had the basic questions of a new believer. People were trying to give my life a specific definition, and I was still in awe over the fact that God loved me. I was over-whelmed just to know Him and serve Him, even in the smallest ways. I do remember being amazed at the ways God seemed to be letting me know He could use me, if I were willing. I also kept finding biblical examples of people called by God to fully trust and obey, long before they were given all the details. I simply wanted to follow Jesus and let Him decide where to place me and how to use me. I came to realize that the priority was cultivating an inti-mate love relationship with my Heavenly Father. He convinced me that by being flexible, available and teachable, He would allow me to join Him in His worldwide work.

Academically, I pursued two programs in Bible College. I took courses in both the pastoral ministry and intercultural studies. My undergraduate degree bears the title "Bachelor of Arts." In essence, I studied the Bible as well as ways to communicate its truths cross-culturally. In spite of many opportunities to preach and the predictions that I was destined to be a preacher, the persistent passion I felt always flared up in my cross-cultural anthropology classes. My heart longed to be the Lord's witness in less-served areas where there was little light shining—to be "a flame on the front line."

**Panama Bunch**

During the summer of 1991, I participated in a trip to Panama, sponsored by The International Mission Board of Free Will Baptists. This was my first oppor-tunity to leave the United States and enter another culture. The purpose was to gain exposure and experience various ministries in a cross-cultural setting. I stayed with an American family that was serving the community in and through the local churches of Parita and Chitre. I assisted the family by ministering to their children and helping them with their home-schooling. I also joined Pastor Stan Bunch and the local brothers and sisters with construction projects, a tamale-making venture, and various activities with young people. It was a joy to help address community needs in the name of the Lord Jesus Christ. My Spanish speaking skills soared along the way, and the whole summer turned out to be a very positive experience.

The day I was scheduled to fly from Panama City back to the States we were robbed. While checking in at the airport an official told me my passport needed some stamp from one of the "Government Offices." It sounded exactly like what I now often hear in Afghanistan. Anyway, we exited the airport and drove quickly to obtain this stamp. While waiting a total of nine minutes in the government office, we returned to the vehicle to find that everything was stolen. What really broke my heart was that they even took my Bible. I do not know if they ever read it, but I do know that God wrote something in my spirit during my first cross-cultural trip. I returned to the States with only a pair of handmade leather sandals and a Panamanian shirt. I was even more convinced, however, that my desire to serve cross-culturally fit my sense of calling from God. I thought, "This work is cool and I love it."

**Kurds Are Coming**

That fall God inspired us to expand some of our Christian service ministries at FWBBC. First, we noticed that thousands of international students were studying in Nashville. We prayed that God might allow us to serve them. Also, thousands of Kurdish families who were exiles from Iraq during the Gulf War were arriving for resettlement in the United States. A number of churches in the Nashville area were gearing up to welcome them. I remember being impressed by the outpouring of concern and openness that God's Spirit stirred in those churches. I heard many believers in a number of these fellowships, like Belmont Church, repeatedly express that God had somehow designated Nashville as a city of refuge for these refugees. To some this sounded strange, but it was very prophetic. God was bringing the nations, unreached peoples, to Nashville!

The Iraqi Kurdish families I worked with introduced me to Middle Eastern culture, the practices of Islam, and the whole idea of refugee ministry. I became an active volunteer with the agencies that were involved in this resettlement project—World Relief, Catholic Charities, and Servant Group International. They matched individual volunteers with specific Kurdish families. We had various practical duties: driving lessons, conversational English classes, job placement, and how to go shopping.

One day at the grocery store, my new Muslim friend, Mohammed, and I were practicing the names of various products. As we walked and talked, Mohammed held my hand. He was not gay. In fact, he had a wife and seven children at home. In his part of the world, men hold hands as a sign of pure friendship. So do the women. Here I was, learning Middle Eastern culture in aisle seven of the grocery store. At that time I could not go to "the regions beyond," but God in His sovereignty brought some from "the ends of the earth" to my doorstep.

I adopted Mohammed's family, and they adopted me. In the process of giving them specific assistance as they settled into American culture, I also got to practice some of the principles of cross-cultural communication that I had been learning in school. I worked on a new language and the challenges of sharing my life with a family whose worldview was drastically different from mine. I participated in cultural picnics and other gatherings. They literally pulled me into their dances and welcomed me at their tables. My Kurdish family took great delight in dressing me for those occasions.

The challenge of building bridges of integrity and friendship that might eventually allow me to share the Gospel strongly attracted me. The possibility of working with Muslims seemed like an invitation to travel in an uncharted and largely unexplored frontier in which I could serve God. In the meantime, God had brought the world to Nashville, and I was eager to learn as much as possible. At this point, going to Afghanistan had not yet entered the picture.

My exposure to the Kurds in my own country had me dreaming about living among people like them in their native lands. The Kurds were an unreached Muslim people group. I did entertain the thought of traveling to Iraq. But God had other plans. The first Islamic country that caught my attention turned out to be Libya. I was reading articles and books by people like Bob Sjogrun, Don Richardson, and Ralph Winter—all pioneers in cross-cultural ministry.

Bob Sjogrun visited Nashville to teach a course on the central theme of the Bible. For me it was the big picture, an unforgettable journey from Creation to the Book of Revelation. The voyage started with "In the beginning," on to "the fall" and then a beautiful view of the Redemptive Promise of Genesis 3:15. There we see the first prophecy of the coming Messiah who will crush the serpent. Later, we looked at the story of Noah, the Flood, and the Tower of Babel as the human race went from a single language to 70 in one sovereign touch of the tongue.

We refer to this linguistic act of God, "confusing their languages" as the creation of nations, which are ethnic groups or people groups who speak the same mother tongue. It is helpful to understand that while there are 220-some countries (e.g., Afghanistan) there are now thousands of nations or ethnic groups (e.g., Pashtuns). Another example is the people group, the Cherokee Indians, who live in the United States of America. Then Bob camped out at God's covenant promise to Abraham, "I will bless all the families of the earth," where he built a foundation for God's heart for every nation (ethnos) or people group.

### 67th Psalm

I, like many others, was surprised to see God's heart for the nations in every book of the Bible.

Even when Jehovah God providentially put a plan in place to build the Jewish temple, He reminded his chosen people that other nations would also come and worship. This desire of God was echoed in the temple as the children of Israel regularly recited the Old Testament scriptures.

Hear Psalm 67, "May God be merciful and bless us. May His face smile with favor on us. May Your ways be known throughout the earth, Your saving power among people everywhere. May the nations praise You, O God. Yes, may all the nations praise You."

Our biblical route led us onward to the coming of Christ and the outpouring of the Holy Spirit on the church, and finally to the role call of nations in the book of Revelation. All these passages and others established a solid theology that represented the seamless story of God's global plan for the redemption of every tribe, nation, kindred and language. This teaching, coupled with the love verse of John 3:16, began to increasingly remind me that "whosoever believes" meant people *everywhere* needed to hear this wonderful story of the Bible. We must reach every people group with the Gospel!

As Bob presented the material of his book, *Destination 2000*, he continually mentioned experiences he had while serving in Libya. He inspired several of us with the needs of that country. He arrived on the scene when my life overflowed with desire and motivation, but lacked a specific target. It was not hard to convince me, the young zealous disciple, who wanted to set out where no one has gone before.

Libya seemed as good a frontier as any. I was ready to go. Unfortunately, the ways and means did not materialize, and the dream of going to Libya faded. The passion to serve, however, remained strong and continued to burn as I pressed on with my studies at FWBBC.

# Chapter 7

# Goen Hall

The family atmosphere at FWBCC fostered enduring friendships. Living in community is not always easy, but that is our calling. Christianity is all about relationships. At the heart of them we find such qualities as love, trust, unity, respect, communication and the list goes on. If we look at God the Father, God the Son, God the Holy Spirit, we see holy love, perfect unity, complete trust, mutual respect and open communication. In the Trinity we see a divine team relationship that is not only absolutely worthy of our worship, but also replication and imitation.

Campus life was perfect for me, despite the fact that I still struggled with being away from my family. I loved FWBBC; however, there were times when my heart drifted back to North Carolina. When asked to share a prayer request, mainly I mentioned my family. In my own "prayer closet," I spent a lot of time on my knees in prayer, weeping in intercession for my mom, sisters and, most of all, my brother, Jerry. One day, there was a note stuck on my door. "John, please call home" was written on the small yellow paper. My heart dropped as I read it, for I sensed something was wrong. I called my mom and heard her tearful voice say, "Your brother Jerry tried to commit suicide again." Not knowing if he would live or die, I immediately made plans to travel home.

## Black River

My brother's drug addiction was hard on our family. We all loved him dearly, but at times we almost gave up hope. God never did. Our Heavenly Father always loves, for *GOD is LOVE*. Even though Jerry tried to take his life several times, God kept him alive. One day, amazing grace won the victory. God miraculously changed Jerry as he repented and made restitution for his wrongdoing. Jerry realized, however, that he needed professional help to fully break the cocaine chain. Together as a family, we took Jerry to Fellowship Hall Treatment Center in Greensboro, North Carolina. But who would pay for it? Who could pay for it? Divorced parents, single mom, sisters still in grade school, drug addict brother: all eyes were on me.

I was working three jobs to pay tuition at FWBBC. In total, my strenuous workweek provided a good chunk of change for a 19 year old. Oh, did I wrestle with the Lord. I told God, "I would die for my brother, but I cannot give him my school money." Well, God broke my heart and wallet when I wrote a check for $1,000 to Fellowship Hall. Please understand, my tuition fee arranged by Mr. Tom Sass, the financial director of FWBBC, was $580 monthly and I was still making payments on the Mitsubishi Precis. For me, every penny counted. Now I was more than two months behind.

At the treatment center, my brother was transformed into a new person, a complete overhaul. He should write a before-and-after story. Also, while at home in Coats, the Spirit of God touched my little sister, Sandi Lynn. Tears rolled down my eyes one night, as we knelt beside her bed, because she wanted to accept Jesus Christ as her Savior. God is always at work. Soon I forgot about the check for $1,000 and returned to Nashville. But would FWBBC allow me to continue my studies without paying?

God in His wisdom sent me on a student preaching trip. Often, certain students are asked to visit other churches to represent the college. These were wonderful opportunities to share the Word of God and gain ministry experience. I loved these journeys. For me, it was also a time to meet other followers of Jesus and get some fresh air from the normal FWBBC fish bowl. My stop was Black River, South Carolina. As usual, I preached my heart out. I passionately and persuasively challenged the believers at Black River to greater love, unity, holiness and outreach. I also encouraged them with stories of God's love and faithfulness.

At the close of the message, I gave a normal altar call. Some did respond and came forward for prayer. The miracle of the day, however, was about to happen in me. At the last "Amen," God sent Brother

Donald Smith my way. He stood tall like Sampson. His hands were huge. He tenderly thanked me for sharing the Word and then squeezed my hand firmly. As he let go, he left something in my palm. I carefully put it in my pocket and said, "Thank you."

In a typical Baptist church, we mingle or "fellowship" together before departing, which sometimes lasts longer than the service. Later, as I left Black River, I remembered putting something in my pocket. Astonished, I read the check made out for $1,000. I shed tears and shouted praise to God! Because He showed His faithfulness in a very personal way, I have never doubted God's financial provision. I have many other struggles, but this is not one of them. God proved Himself. I must simply trust and obey. By the way, after my brother got back on his feet, he insisted on repaying the $1,000. Talk about a double blessing!

**Roomies**

I want to mention a few others from Goen Hall. Since I had transferred from Campbell, I only had one semester with my first roommate, Dewey. He influenced me with his quiet, yet godly personality. Russell, my second roommate, was from Arkansas. I recall his passion for cycling and the cause of Christ. Do you remember Fellowship Free Will Baptist Church back in Dunn, North Carolina? A good friend from that youth group, Tim Killingsworth, also attended FWBBC. God arranged for us to share a room and even today we still share a special bond. My most memorable roomie was Sean Warren. He could have written this chapter because he tells hilarious stories about our season together.

I had just returned from my summer trip to Panama, when Sean set foot on campus. He made a grand entrance because of his tall stature and extremely loud car speakers. His main desire was to play basketball for the *Flames*, our school's collegiate team. I think he also wanted some freedom from home and a chance to show off his car speakers, which shook the windows of Goen Hall. As Sean entered the dormitory that day he was welcomed by two popular upperclassmen, Kenny Simpson and Rod Goodman. They looked at the list and laughingly told Sean, "Your roommate is John Weaver." This disappointed Sean who was hoping to have a cool roommate who already knew the ropes.

Remember all my belongings, including my Bible, were stolen in Panama. On the other hand I was fired up about overseas work. On the day we met I was wearing handmade leather sandals, a sheer Panamanian shirt and a straw hat. Sean thought I was a bit strange and soon started questioning God's sovereignty. He was afraid his Jesus-freak roommate would spoil the fun of his freshman year.

Sean and I became close friends. Perhaps it is easy when you share the same room for a year. Indeed, our Father did give us many communal experiences. Most are unforgettable. Once, while I was sleeping, Sean took hairspray and painted a cross on the wall above my bed. Next he struck a match and lit the hairspray. Then he frantically shook me screaming "Holy fire." Startled out of my wits to see the blazing cross above my head, I almost wet the bed. Meanwhile, Sean grew to respect me as an older brother and even looked up to me, although I was a foot shorter. We talked often about serious issues and being fully committed to following the Lord Jesus Christ.

At one point in our relationship I was truly concerned for Sean. I began praying specifically for him, every day. We also often prayed together in our room, and one night I asked Sean, "Man, are there any idols in your life?" Sean was not offended or surprised by the straight-forward question. His reply mentioned his expensive car speakers. A few hours later we woke to a knock on our door. It was the night security guard, who told Sean his car had been burglarized. Guess what they stole! You got it: his car speakers. Sean would go on to graduate, marry his college sweetheart, Jill, and father three beautiful daughters. He is faithfully serving the Lord today as "a flame on the front line."

For the majority of us who attended FWBBC, one of the most difficult experiences was saying good-bye to so many special brothers and sisters. I felt separation anxiety and shed many tears when I left Nashville. Since I was still young and unsure about the future, I thought more training might be helpful. After I graduated in May 1993, I explored other avenues to be furthered sharpened for long-term service.

## Stan the Man

This pursuit led me to a graduate studies program with the University of Texas (UTA). I made a whole new set of friends, improved my social skills and studied linguistics and anthropology from January 1994 until May 1995. Texas was another great stop on "preparation highway."

While in Texas I found a population of Kurdish refugees, an Arabic-speaking Christian Fellowship, and thousands of international students at UTA. God used all of these connections to further school me. He even allowed us to have a ministry at UTA, where we gave free copies of the Holy Bible to interested students. Imagine! There were at least 65 languages spoken at UTA and we had scripture portions of God's Word in 63 of them. What an open door right in our front and back yards. Oh, the depths and the riches of the wisdom of God, whose work in the world is sometimes mysterious! Indeed, His ways are not our ways.

Then I discovered Central Asia, the vast area that stretches from Turkey to China and encompasses all the "stans." The "stan" that is part of the names of all these countries stands for "land," so Afghanistan means Land of the Afghans. Most of these countries are known for their poverty, illiteracy and other major humanitarian problems. They are also full of unreached peoples and Bible-less language groups. I even met various students from most of the "stans" while studying at UTA.

At this time in history, communism had just collapsed. The "stans" were stepping out of their suppressive shadows and into the 20th century. Many of them were suddenly open: Kazakhstan, Kyrgyzstan, Tajikistan, Turkmenistan, and Uzbekistan. Even countries like Afghanistan, Iran, Pakistan, and Turkey, which had not been in the Soviet Bloc, gained new attention from the rest of the world. These names were on everyone's lips and began to permeate our prayers. God put a love in my heart for them, which burns like a continual flame.

These Central Asian countries include people groups that had never had the opportunity to hear the Good News of Jesus Christ. There were dozens of languages that had never been written down. Though the Islamic nature of these countries represented challenges and restrictions to the work of Christians, the apparent needs offered unlimited opportunities for service. In the field of linguistics and anthropology, there were requests for proper surveys to determine the exact number of languages and their relationships to each other, population counts, literacy assessments and translation needs.

I could not think of one reason not to pursue these opportunities of humanitarian assistance. I became part of an informal group that was focusing on the linguistic needs of Central Asia. We met daily to pray for these nations. I felt burdened by the immense humanitarian needs of the "stans": the tyranny and persecution in Turkmenistan, the oppression and darkness in Uzbekistan, the civil war and poverty of Tajikistan. My heart, however, was particularly drawn to Afghanistan, one of the few countries still without one Christian church. Something or someone was beckoning me to come and help in this part of the planet.

We began making preparations to pave the way for us to enter Central Asia after our training. We hoped to conduct linguistic surveys, cataloguing the various dialects and languages spoken in the area. Few efforts to get the Gospel into many areas of Central Asia had ever been attempted. The frontier challenges and pioneer instincts were calling out to me. Why not go on the road less traveled? The more I learned about the needs in Afghanistan and prayed and wept for its peoples, the more I wanted to travel on the Silk Road.

**Weaverville**

Throughout this time in my life, a special group of people, supporting and serving in the background, were cheering me on. They still do today. Back in 1991, while staying at Geon Hall, I was invited to speak at a regional youth rally in western North Carolina. This was arranged by the college's development department, like the preaching tours mentioned earlier. I am not sure why they picked me for this one. I recall when Ronald Creech and Bob Shockey told me about the trip. They were the same two brothers who planned the journey for me down to Black River, South Carolina. They mentioned that the weekend activities would also include preaching at a church in Weaverville.

I thought the invitation for John Weaver to preach in *Weaverville* might be a joke. Instead of looking at a map, I started daydreaming about such a place. Then

Brother Bob Shockey, nicknamed God's wildcat, said with a big smile, "You're going to preach, Boy. Not only that, but we want you to represent the college at this Weaverville church." It had been years since a representative from FWBBC had spoken there. God was stirring the congregation, which had recently shown some signs of interest in supporting the college and other Christian works around the world. Off I went to find Weaverville!

Do you want to guess what my first sermon at Mt. Bethel Free Will Baptist Church in Weaverville was? I preached about "God's heart for the nations." What I lacked in experience, I compensated with zeal and enthusiasm. I used the concepts I had learned from classes, books, and speakers to explain the biblical principle, "Blessed to be a blessing." I told them that an unbroken thread woven through the Scriptures is that God is in the business of blessing His children, so that they become His channel to bless the nations of the world. The 67th Psalm best illustrates this by showing us that God has mercy on us and blesses us, so that His ways may be known on the earth and that His salvation may spread to all nations. It portrays all the peoples (ethnos or nations) praising God for His greatness!

I must admit, until I saw the town signs, I wasn't sure about this Weaverville thing. It sounded like a fairy tale. I knew nothing about the church. Yet God allowed my message to bring a fresh perspective to a discussion that had weighed upon that congregation. They had been struggling and wrestling over the decision to give a significant amount of money to help build churches in China. Some had been raising the issue of priorities: "Do we take care of needs here at home, or do we help meet the needs in other parts of the world?" They were facing a dilemma most churches must resolve at some point.

That Sunday I did preach. I passionately shared what was in my heart and how God's truth was transforming my life. In trying to show them God's heart for the nations, I unknowingly helped them look at their own hearts. God's sovereignty was demonstrated to me in an exciting way, when I discovered that the message flowing from my heart was the timely word from the Lord that they needed to hear. This small congregation in the mountains of western North Carolina realized that giving $20,000 was nothing compared to God's blessings to them. This kind of sharing illustrated the main point of the message: "We are blessed to be a blessing." This church decided to learn firsthand the reality of this eternal kingdom principle.

Some families from the church took me out for lunch that Sunday. They asked how I felt about working with young people. By the time we had dessert, they were offering me a job as youth pastor in the church. I remember thinking, "John Weaver in Weaverville—could this be a sign?" As flattering as the offer was, I first needed to finish FWBBC and then be sent out to do pioneering work overseas. Although I gently turned down their offer, my connection with Mt. Bethel Church continued to develop in the months to come. Weaverville was definitely on the map!

The pastor, Roy McPeters, made a serious request of me. Since Weaverville was close to Asheville, the midway point between Nashville and Raleigh, I should visit when traveling. That began a series of occasional contacts in which the church and I got to know one another better. I spoke at youth events, preached on Sundays, and sometimes just visited. This relationship developed throughout the rest of my time at FWBBC and UTA.

In the summer of 1995, I received an invitation to work at the church, between school semesters. Since this recurring invitation from Weaverville was so persuasive, I agreed to come. My conditions were: to be a volunteer, live with a family in the church, and receive no salary. They told me I drove a hard bargain. By the end of that summer, I felt as if I had found a long-term church family. Although I was an outsider entering a small, rural community, they adopted me like their own son, and the leadership in that church began to exercise some helpful spiritual authority in my life.

Weaverville was, indeed, a real place. The believers there had a huge influence on my life. Between 1995 and 1996 the leadership of the church approached me again with the following counsel: "John, we know that you plan to serve overseas, but God is still equipping you in many ways. We'd like you to consider being part of our church staff for an ongoing relationship for as long as you are in the States." With that, Mt. Bethel Free Will Baptist Church became my home base.

I had wonderful opportunities to learn, grow and get firsthand ministry experience. The way God ordained the situation and relationship was absolutely brilliant. During the next several years, the congregation and community graciously supported me as I pursued various opportunities to gain experience overseas. When I preached that first sermon about how God blesses us in order to be a blessing to others, I had no idea that I would receive such blessings from that church. Weaverville turned out to be Heaven's storehouse for me. God is not only supreme—He has a great sense of humor!

**Off to the Islands**

In January 1997, I flew to the Philippines for a field course. One of the requirements of our study program was to participate in an overseas assignment that involved linguistic and anthropological research and community development. The courses at UTA had focused on the academic side; this experience was to expose us to the practical aspects of living and working in another culture.

Four of us from Texas joined 25 other participants in the field course. After successful completion, our foursome intended to serve somewhere in Central Asia. We stayed in the Philippines three months. We "got our feet wet" doing introductory language learning, culture adaptation and conducting community development projects. This was intense, supervised, on-the-job training. Each of us received continuous performance evaluations. Every aspect of our lives was scrutinized to better prepare us for the rigors of living under the microscope of another culture.

I probably enjoyed it too much. I settled in and started to plant myself. I was learning with good friends and seeing my dream of serving in another culture come true. I lived in a handmade bamboo hut on an island with the Rambusa family, who hosted me. Mountains filled our back yard, and our front yard was the beach. Arsenio, the father of the family, often took me net-fishing in the ocean. Coconut juice and papaya fruit made up our afternoon snack. He also taught me to climb coconut trees and walk in the mountains. Unfortunately, my feet were not as tough as his, so I had blisters most of the time. Yet this experience was like paradise.

The Rambusa family passionately loved Jesus. Recently, they had come to know Him as the Way, the Truth and the Life. As some of the few believers who spoke the local Visayan dialect, they were eager to share their faith with their extended family and neighbors. It was special to be with Uncle Arsenio when he told others about his relationship with the Messiah. Since their alphabet was Roman-based, he let me read portions of God's Word, though I didn't understand much. I worked hard at building relationships and language learning, even though my stay was short-term.

I felt right at home in the Rambusas' hut and I learned heaps. One day, I stepped out of the door to put on my sandals. I wanted another chance to climb the coconut tree. Since the soles of my feet were sore, it seemed wise to wear shoes. After searching and searching, however, I could not find them. Then I realized Asian culture is community oriented as I saw Arsenio's wife, Lette, wearing my sandals. I quietly slipped on another pair that was next to the door. Off I went to the garden.

Suddenly, I heard an awful sound. It was Arsenio's cow tumbling down the side of the mountain. It practically landed at my feet. I started crying, knowing that this cow was their livelihood. Staring at the bleeding unconscious cow, something burned in me like a flame of fire and I laid hands on it and prayed in the mighty name of Jesus. The cow instantly stood up. Oh, the depths of God's mercy!

Soon I was asked to share a testimony at the local fellowship. I was glad to speak of His salvation and work in my life. As the last week of our assignment approached, they asked me again. This time the request was for me to share a message from the Word of God. What an opportunity to share about God's heart for the nations. I was enjoying this participation so much; some thought my actions unusual and unexpected. This was field training, not necessarily a ministry time.

My supervisors were concluding that I might fit better as a teaching evangelist than a researching linguist. They said I was more of a hands-on worker than a secluded scholar. I had demonstrated excellent language-learning abilities, but they wondered how I would handle the long and tedious work of language analysis. The tentative plan was still to leave the Philippines for an extensive language survey in Central Asia; however, the visas we needed to travel in that area never materialized. We were stuck. I actually considered staying in the Philippines. But was that God's will for me?

To debrief and unwind a bit, we visited the Catholic Retreat Center in Bagio City. This also gave us some time alone to rest and renew. I told God: "Oh, Father, thanks for this time of stillness and quietness. I really want to seek You. I'm not going to eat normal meals, but spend the extra time with You instead." Seven days into the fast, as I was alone in my room, kneeling beside the bed, I had the most moving experience. I'm not certain whether to call it a dream or a vision. What I visualized was obvious, yet overwhelming and almost unbelievable. I saw myself serving in Afghanistan, the land of my dreams. God in a supernatural way refocused me and reminded me of the journey. It was a sweet surprise that totally confirmed His call on my life!

As the practical field course ended, I had no visa for Central Asia. Neither did my other buddies who had their sights in the same direction. Several of the guys I hoped to work with, followed God's lead through other open doors to Southeast Asia. I phoned my support team at Mt. Bethel for their counsel. Praise God for technology, because on the other end of the line I received helpful guidance. They did not sense that the Philippines fit my passion as a long-term assignment. I told them about the evaluation from the field training staff, and they agreed that God's purposes for me involved more of an applied, relational teaching ministry. They encouraged me to return to Weaverville and wait for God's timing. I appreciated their wisdom and flew home.

I later met with the UTA staff in Texas. They were convinced God was indeed leading me into cross-cultural service, but they discerned and decided that linguistic research was not the best match for me. Our official relationship ended at that meeting. I still have deep respect for them and their work worldwide. Although the decision was painful, it was purposeful. Nothing was wasted, for God used this experience to further refine me and ignite the flame in my heart. I am grateful for the training, the relationships built, and the faithful examples of the faculty. This was another strategic stop en route to Afghanistan. Yes, Texas treated me well!

# Chapter 8

# Live and Learn

The outcome of the expedition to the Philippines was not expected. Afghanistan seemed farther away than ever. The road was bumpy and filled with what seemed to be potholes and detours. My friends from Texas were no longer nearby. I was now in the States with no means to get anywhere near the "stans." These events, and others, were engineered by God to test me, try my patience and further equip me. I didn't come out like pure gold in God's fiery furnace. He did skim some of the impurities from my life, but I'm still in the Refiner's fire. It is true that, with our minds we plan our path, but God directs our steps.

This reminds me of one our women's projects in Western Afghanistan. Over the years, we have started many programs from scratch, but also inherited worthy endeavors from others. One excellent business enterprise God recently dropped into our lap is a Ladies Jewelry Project. Every time I see Afghan women using their skills it brings me to tears.

This small jewelry project is no different. It was a joy to witness their work, buy their finished products and send them to the States as Christmas presents. These beautiful gifts were for the other women in my life: my mom, sisters, nieces and sister-in-law. Their favorite piece of jewelry was one designed with pearls. Think about oysters: slimy, stinky and sticky. Now rub your fingers around your neck and feel a soft, elegant pearl necklace. Remember how pearls are produced from oysters the next time you face some unexpected or unwanted irritation in your life.

God-ordained trials are necessary preparation for greater service. They are life lessons. Bends in the road are a catalyst to take us to new heights. Transition or disappointment can cause us to draw closer to the Lord. Their purpose is to focus us on the process of becoming more and more like Him. Our culture teaches us to run from trials and stay far from suffering. The Word of God, however, is clear that trials are designed to rid us of selfishness and mature us into godliness. We are to count it all joy when we face difficulties, because our faith, worth more than gold, is being purified. I have included various stories to illustrate that there is hope for each day, joy in the journey, grace for every season, and usually surprises along the way.

The Bible says, "Therefore, since we have been made right in God's sight by faith, we have peace with God because of what Jesus Christ our Lord has done for us. Because of our faith, Christ has brought us into this place of undeserved privilege where we now stand, and we confidently and joyfully look forward to sharing God's glory. We can rejoice, too, when we run into problems and trials, for we know that they help us develop endurance. And endurance develops strength of character, and character strengthens our confident hope of salvation. And this hope will not lead to disappointment. For we know how dearly God loves us, because He has given us the Holy Spirit to fill our hearts with His love." (Romans 5:1-5).

After returning from the Philippines, I enjoyed the opportunities to teach and preach at my home base in Weaverville. Yet at times I said: "Father God, what is up with all of this? I mean, I love it here but when are You going to send me to Afghanistan?" In the meantime, God was building me and a team around me. I would desperately need the daily prayer coverage of the saints and their continual involvement to make it for the long term inside Afghanistan.

I got to know people from the church in deeper ways, and they got to know me better. Mutual respect and reciprocal support is a rare and treasured commodity in our modern, fast paced world. I was "adopted" by many families as a result of the Weaverville connection. Along with building community relationships and pastoral responsibilities at Mt. Bethel, there was also the freedom to pursue both international ministries and educational opportunities. This Weaverville context created a preparation ground par excellence!

**A Volvo of a View**

God in His sovereign plan brought a community of Russian immigrants to the Asheville area of Western North Carolina. Some of them actually found us in Weaverville, at Mt. Bethel Free Will Baptist Church. Thanks to a graduate course back at UTA, I could speak about two minutes' worth of Russian. Here right in my backyard, God arranged some beautiful relationships with the Russian community. He allowed me to form such a unique bond with the Gundorin family that in the summer of 1997 we journeyed together to Germany, Eastern Europe, Belarus, and Russia. Vladimir, the father of the family, was concerned about his Russian brothers and sisters around the world and wanted me to go with his family to some of them.

Our trip was more than a vacation. It turned out to be full of divine appointments and service opportunities. Our first stop was the small community of Blankenshire, Germany, home to many Russian refugees. I had the privilege of sharing in the little Russian Pentecostal Church there. It was unusual, not because of the language or style of worship, but for another reason. I often spoke these words: "Because Russia invaded Afghanistan, you need to ask for forgiveness. God wants to mobilize a new army from Russia and the former Soviet Union to pray for Afghanistan and send workers there on a mission of mercy. Do you understand what I'm saying? Don't shoot me down now! Ask God to send Russian believers to Afghanistan, armed not with guns and tanks, but with the Word of God and His Spirit of love. Are you with me?" I learned later that my fellow co-worker, Vladimir, was not fully with me, if you know what I mean. He wasn't sure how Afghanistan and our summer journey connected.

I was introduced to that part of the planet "at ground level." We traveled in a Volvo through Germany and then Belarus. What a warm welcome I received at one the Russian Baptist Churches we visited. Brother Vladimir elaborately introduced me and, as I walked to the pulpit, I was kissed on the lips several times by the elders of the church. As a single guy I do not get kissed a lot. The Bible does say, "Greet one another with a holy kiss." But this was a first.

Again in my message to the church I mentioned Afghanistan and my vision of going to this needy land to share God's love in word and deed. Where are the servants of our Lord Jesus Christ who will go? I told them, "God wants you to pray for the people of Afghanistan! Are you with me?" It was still hard to know if anyone agreed with me. Only God knew.

We spent many long days in that Volvo. Russia is a vast country. Vladimir and I took turns driving to maximize our journey. We sang, prayed, ate and slept all along the way. Finding gasoline led us to unusual places, but eventually we arrived in Southwest Russia, near the Caucasus Mountains. God was up to something in this small area of Russia. The house church that Vladimir had helped start several years earlier was doing well.

**One in the Spirit**

How is the larger body of Christ doing? Jesus' Church is made up of a variety of followers. It is kind of like eating at a restaurant. Ever noticed how a church bulletin reflects a dinner menu? If you were to ask 100 people, "Where do you want to eat?" you would not get the same answer. Even if you did, there would be great debate about what to eat and how it should be cooked. The worldwide Christian family functions the same way. All born again believers are the children of God, sealed by the Holy Spirit and instructed to endeavor to keep the unity of the Spirit. Of course, we are different in personality, background, language and culture. Yes, this makes it difficult to get along. If we focus on our differences, we miss the simple joys of serving Jesus and living in harmony with one another. When the redeemed of Christ lovingly unite at the Cross, we bring Him great pleasure and the world takes notice!

In Southern Russia, God let us join in with Him on a few important assignments. First, He wanted to break down some religious walls. The three main churches in this area are Baptist, Charismatic and Pentecostal. They all have strengths and weaknesses like every other Christian place of worship on the planet. Though very much divided, they have a common concern for the needs of their communities. Thus we called a joint meeting to pray and see how God would want us to minister to the community.

I shared with my Russian brothers the prayer of our Lord Jesus in John 17. Jesus asked for love and unity among His followers, because that would cause the world to know He is the Messiah. Our Savior asked that we be one, as He and the Father are one. These brothers came face to face with the reality that some of the problems in the community could be traced to their own walls of hostility.

God spoke that night, and all who listened wanted to get their act together. We began with the prayer, "God, what do You want us to do?" A few things came to mind: visit our neighbors and pray with them, minister to the sick at the hospital and have services to share the Good News of Jesus Christ. We were all in agreement and asked God to lead us to a place to meet. In a miraculous way, God provided a stately, old Russian theater that later became the property of one of the local churches. Every night God brought people to hear Vladimir and me. Why? As outsiders with wide local support, we had the unique opportunity to speak about Jesus Christ to the wider community. By working together in unity, more was accomplished.

## Miracles

One day, several of us went to a dilapidated hospital to visit the sick. My Russian was still limited to a greeting and a few phrases. I relied on our team to share the Word of God. Vladimir served as my translator when I had something to say. Most of our time was spent in prayer for the sick. There was no medicine and very little health care. The hospital was cold, dingy, dirty, smelly, and many lay suffering. We saw face after face of sadness and hopelessness. But God in His kindness touched a few people as we prayed. I remember two widows that Svetlana, Vladimir's wife, spoke with about the love of Jesus. These ladies left the hospital healed that day and came to the nightly service. They are now both faithful servants of the Lord Jesus. Wow, talk about God confirming His Word with miracles!

My mind frequently drifted to Afghanistan during those days in Russia. When I spoke at the services in the movie theater, I frequently asked people to pray for Afghanistan. I couldn't shake this burden and it was obvious to all around me. I also realized I was asking them to do something very difficult. The Russians had been humiliated by the Afghans and there remained a lot of hidden animosity.

There were times when Vladimir did pray specifically for the needs of Afghanistan. Some even began to say, "John is right! We need to ask God for forgiveness for what our country did. We should pray for peace in Afghanistan. We should all extend grace to others and join this mission of mercy." How refreshing it was to see that some were finally with me. Our journey almost over, we left the Volvo as a present for a local pastor. Shortly, we would set out on the long flight back to Charlotte, North Carolina.

Back in the States, I settled into my own bed. I was living with the Ponder family in their basement. Their large, three-story house on the hill was known as the "Ponderosa." Though I had no family in Weaverville, God daily provided and encouraged me through others, who prayed, gave and supported. The Ponders are only one example among a hundred other families that have "adopted me." This has been

God's pattern everywhere I go. My life is deeply enriched to have so many caring friends all over the planet.

I am reminded of the words of Jesus, who often had no place to lay his head, when He said, "Everyone who has given up houses or brothers or sisters or father or mother or children or property, for My sake, will receive a hundred times as much in return and will inherit eternal life." (Matthew 19: 26).

## Habla Espanol?

Time and again, God so extended my borders and enlarged my territory by divine networks from the little town of Weaverville. His ways of making me a blessing far exceeded my desire to be one. In August 1997, God linked me with a group from Gateway Community in Asheville, North Carolina. I was introduced to these new friends by one of the brothers at Mt. Bethel. They invited me to be part of a summer trip to Guatemala in South America. Our primary objective was a building project in San Andreas. What a joy to work, to sweat, to serve together! We enjoyed such unity, had wonderful times of worship and opportunities to share our love for Jesus Christ with that Spanish-speaking community. For me it was one more sovereign step into the nations!

"Back at the ranch" in Weaverville, I meet with the elders and deacons at Mt. Bethel Church in September 1997. I was not sure of the next step, but they had some wise counsel to give. Since I had not officially finished my Master of Arts degree at UTA, they encouraged me to do so. Also, since

I had previously mentioned an interest in studying at Columbia International University in Columbia, South Carolina, they gave me their blessing to finish my M.A. there. Columbia was just over two hours away, so I could come home and serve at the church on weekends. I thought, "Oh, God, this is marvelous, You are so good! Your timing is perfect. Thanks again for another dream come true!"

**Grad School**

I began almost immediately to take correspondence courses from Columbia. They were convenient and allowed me to stay in Weaverville. Since the Seminary accepted all my previous courses from UTA, I was only asked to spend one full semester on campus for the residency requirement. From January to May 1998, I studied hard and received a Master of Arts in Intercultural Studies. It was an academic accomplishment. Even more than the degree, I valued the experience, the relationships, and being in the right place at the right time for another strategic step into the nations.

Speaking of the nations, many experiences in Columbia helped focus my attention on regions far beyond. I remember reading *In Step with the God of the Nations* by one of my professors, Dr. Steyne and *Let the Nations Be Glad* by Dr. John Piper. These books took me further in my journey of understanding God's plan for the universe. Reading them caused me to review and relive what I learned in Nashville, Panama, Texas and the Philippines. I was on the right track.

Soon God showed me, again, that He had brought the peoples of the earth to America for His purposes. One of my roommates was ethnic Chinese. Now he and his Korean wife serve in Southeast Asia. I also helped several Arab and African students with their English. Hanging out with friends from the Middle East and Central Asia was both fun and fulfilling. Yet would God ever send me to the nations?

One of my favorite sayings is, "Prayer is where it's at!" At Columbia there were various ways that God fueled our prayer life as students. Every Thursday Dr. Ed Cheek and his wife, Dr. Nancy Cheek, opened up their home for a Central Asia Prayer Meeting. We gathered and expressed known concerns for the "stans" of the world. After the sharing we would "go to prayer," as Brother Ed liked to say. He became a close friend and mentor like the Apostle Paul was to young Timothy. He was an example of "a flame on the front line." He had a burning passion for God and His glory among the Nations. Also, Dr. Warren Larson, one of my professors in the Intercultural Program, encouraged us to pray specifically for the needs of the nations in the Middle East, especially every Friday.

## Culturally Challenged

I loved my classes. They clarified my worldview. One of my anthropology classes was with Dr. Bob Priest. He grew up in Latin American and had a broad understanding of culture and effective ways to communicate cross-culturally. One day, we divided into groups to role-play. We were each given a particular scenario and had to act it out based on our assigned culture. It was remarkable to see how differently Indians, Americans, Chinese, Aussies, Brits, Africans and Afghans would act or react in the same situation. I knew then that I must become a better student of culture. Maybe the Apostle Paul was on to something when he said; "I become all things to all people in order to share the Good News of Jesus Christ with them."

How could I forget that evening class when Dr. Corley asked me to do a demonstration with him? The idea was to show the challenges of communicating to someone from a Muslim perspective. He introduced himself as Mohammed, a student from the Middle East. Then he asked me to "share my faith" with him. When I mentioned that Jesus was the Son of God he interrupted me. "John, do you really believe Almighty God, who created the entire universe, has a wife?"

I said, "No, of course not!" He replied, "Then how can you say God has a son?" His point was clear. Words that communicate in one setting may confuse in another. We must seek to understand the views of others and learn how our Christian lingo is interpreted. It called to mind the times I went fishing with my dad or grandfather. I never caught a bluegill or a brim with a large red artificial worm, and only once did I catch a largemouth bass with a cricket and cane pole. Bait is important. Your approach when fishing for people or fish is crucial. As Christians, our message doesn't change, but the way we deliver it to people depends on our listeners. I needed to learn a bit more about Mohammed's way of thinking and better understand his perception of Christianity before I started fishing in his pond—to put it simply.

**Barriers or Bridges**

Since 9/11 many of us have been scrambling to learn more about Islam or the Muslim religion. I'd like to highlight some of the barriers I have discovered in sharing my faith with those of the Islamic worldview. These comments are based on my experiences with refugees from Africa, the Middle East, international students and the peoples of Central Asia (and also the research of others).

Here is a glance into the mindset of many Muslims: 1) All Americans or Westerners are Christians, but not too serious about holiness, morality or matters of faith; 2) Most Christians are immoral, because premarital sex, adultery, divorce, pornography, murder and abortion occur everyday in the West or America; 3) Since Christians claim to be forgiven in Christ or "saved by God's grace," we think we are free to live as we wish; 4) Personal disciplines like daily worship, bowing in prayer or fasting from food are not important; and 5) Christians are idolatrous, because they worship three gods, which most Muslims think are God the Father, Mary the Mother and Jesus the Son, or even the green god of money.

I cannot address all these misunderstandings now. Some answers, however are found in the pages that follow. You are most welcome to email me at hope4afg@dxpost.com to continue this dialogue. Believe me; we must be able to respond to these

charges if we interact with Muslims. We must over-
come the stereotypes they have about us Christians.
Our greatest spiritual weapons are: a close walk with
God and Christlikeness, prayer and fasting, uncondi-
tional love and childlike faith, compassionate service
and a life of good works. It is also important to learn
to listen with two ears and speak with one mouth,
mostly by asking questions and telling stories.

**Small Group**

At Columbia, an incredible group of guys
became my accountability network. Along this
journey of faith, I have benefited from the interaction and companionship of some great Christian men
and women. Our little band of brothers decided to
encourage one another to memorize the Word of
God.

First, we chose Romans 8. Here is a taste: "So
now there is no condemnation for those who belong
to Christ Jesus. And because you belong to Him, the
power of the life-giving Spirit has freed you from the
power of sin that leads to death. The Law of Moses
was unable to save us because of the weakness of our
sinful nature. So God did what the law could not do.
He sent His own Son in a body like the bodies we
sinners have. And in that body God declared an end to
sin's control over us by giving His Son as a sacrifice
for our sins. He did this so that the just requirement
of the law would be fully satisfied for us, who no
longer follow our sinful nature but instead follow the
Spirit.....And we know that God causes everything
to work together for the good of those who love God

and are called according to His purpose for them. For God knew His people in advance, and He chose them to become like His Son."

The process of memorization, meditation, and discussion together revolutionized our lives. That single chapter of Scripture led us to continually search the rest of God's Word for deeper truth. Together we longed to more fully trust and obey. These friends and others like them have kept me focused, balanced and committed to the task. One of them, also named John, literally "carried" me through the strenuous experience of Comprehensive Exams, a series of tests you must successfully pass before receiving a Master of Arts degree.

## See for yourself

In May 1998, I learned about a team of friends who were going on a survey trip to Turkey, Turkmenistan, and Uzbekistan to explore opportunities for service. My graduate studies were about to end, and I was drawn to this idea of "scouting out the land." The possibility of visiting the border area of Afghanistan was also mentioned. The plan was to go see if Central Asia was for us. Needless to say, I signed up.

The team I joined consisted of various Christian professionals. Two of them were friends and fellow students from my college days, on the same journey with me. They were underclassmen with much spiritual potential. I sought to model the same teachings and passion that other students, mentors and professors had shared with me. The fact that they were still exploring ways they might serve Christ indicated that our united efforts had born some fruit in their lives. The Intercultural Studies Program at FWBBC and the efforts of professors like Brother Eddie Payne and Dr. Miley had impacted our lives and helped direct us in the right direction.

When I met the rest of the team I made it clear that I had a definite plan for joining their group. Yes, the Silk Road—destination Afghanistan! They were going to be in that area. When they mentioned Termiz, Uzbekistan, my heart jumped. Their idea of teaching (most of them had a M.A in Education) did catch my attention. I love to teach, but it was the location that drew me. Termiz is the border city between Uzbekistan and Afghanistan. Though many other ideas and places were mentioned that day, my mind continued to focus on Termiz. My sights were set and the target was in view.

We traveled from west to east across Central Asia—Turkey, Turkmenistan, and Uzbekistan. I loved the region as much as I had dreamed I would. We observed the cultures, noted the similarities and differences within the region, and enjoyed all the exotic sights, sounds and tastes of that part of the planet. Along the way we also helped trained some local instructors in ESL (English as a Second Language). We all had some experience in this. We also interviewed a number of teams that were already serving in the area. We wanted to hear and see first-hand what needs were being met, which ones were not, and how we might join in and help.

We eventually arrived in Termiz, Uzbekistan, by train. As a border-crossing into Afghanistan, the city lived under tight military restrictions. There was lingering tension between Afghanistan and Uzbekistan, since much of the previous Russian military invasion and supply line had run through Termiz. Though open warfare had ended a decade before, and though the Soviet Union was no longer in "official" control, some of the tension and suspicion remained. Foreigners were under careful scrutiny and the area was labeled "security risk." One reason was that the Taliban were near and had already expressed their agenda for conquering the neighboring countries of Afghanistan.

**Riverside View**

We visited Termiz for a week and spent much time at the university there. The faculty arranged a few English classes and a teachers' seminar. As soon as possible, however, we made our way to the border at al-Termizi, a famous Islamic shrine that houses the body of a holy man. As I looked across the river that separated the two countries, my pulse began to race as I saw Afghanistan. I wasn't there yet, but I was close. My heart was already bound to that country in a way I could not explain.

After that intensive seminar, we returned to Tashkent, the capital of the country. Our trip had come to an end. The others on the team, including me, were scheduled to return to the States. While we were debriefing our experience, I presented the idea that I was considering staying in Uzbekistan. The trip had been a great learning exercise, but I was eager to invest myself in people's lives—to start filling some gaps. Besides, I had finished school and had no other commitments or specific reasons to return to the States.

We discussed it and our leader, Brother Jimmy, reluctantly agreed with my motives. He laid out three sensible conditions: I needed the approval of my home church back in Weaverville, I needed to be released by the group that was sponsoring our team, and I needed to be "adopted" by a team already established in the country, which would look out for me and provide a new accountability structure. What he said made perfect sense.

## Divine Partnership

Though free-spirited and adventurous, I realized I needed support. I did agree that it would not be prudent to continue the journey alone. Brother Jimmy's proposal was like a word from God, which, if fulfilled, would provide strategic contacts, appropriate accountability, and a place for teamwork. All three of his requirements were almost immediately met. Pastor Roy and those back at Mt. Bethel were excited about this new opportunity, though it surprised them as much as me. My summer team released me with their blessing and a new team adopted me, believing it to be the will of God.

About this time, we heard of the earthquakes that shook the *Land of Afghans*. A call went out through Central Asia and other parts of the world to come and help. I thought about it, but the timing wasn't right. Instead, I joined a group of teachers that had been preparing to serve at the University of Termiz.

Noncitizens, however, were not permitted to actually live in Termiz. Because of its location on the border, it was a closed city. We began to pray and asked others to join us. Soon we received special permission from Uzbekistan's President Karimov to live as foreigners in Termiz and teach English at the University. I returned to the border of Afghanistan long before I expected. What a wonderful year it was teaching, learning, and tasting Central Asian life, firsthand.

## Get Out!

Restrictions did tighten and we were asked to leave. There were chances during that school year to share our love for the Lord Jesus. I became keenly aware of how sensitive an issue it is in a nation that officially claims a different religion. I frequently visited the border, lifting my hands and praying for peace in Afghanistan. I asked God to open a way for me to go where my heart already seemed to be. I repeatedly asked God for the opportunity to serve Him among the Afghan people. But the door remained closed.

I left Termiz perplexed and disappointed. I felt even more frustration when we learned later why our visas were not renewed. It had little to do with our being foreigners, but because we were Christians. Some officials were afraid that "sharing our lives" would encourage people to want to know about the Messiah. One influential Muslim cleric once said, "Don't read the Bible, for you will become one of its followers." Well, God's Word does claim to be a

"Living Book" with the words of Truth. Thus, it was more than what we said or did not say that got us into "trouble"—it was the way we lived by God's Word. Who was it that said, "We are the only Bible some will ever read"?

When I first learned the reason for our departure, I wanted to defend myself. As an American, I thought we needed to stand up for our rights, and say, "This is not fair!" We had done nothing wrong and were being treated unjustly. Then the words of our Lord Jesus stuck like a knife, "Blessed are those who are persecuted because of righteousness." In a small way, we had experienced how living right doesn't guarantee you a bed of roses or an easy walk in the park.

My surroundings taught me another lesson. I was living in a culture that uses "Inshallah" (Arabic for "If God wills") in almost every conversation. Saint Peter the Apostle wrote, "Remember, it is better to suffer for doing good, if that is what God wants, than to suffer for doing wrong!" (I Peter 3:17) God comforted me with this timeless truth. If it is His will that I "lose out" by doing right, that is good and I should rejoice. My mind was at ease and my conscience clear, even though my good was being spoken of as evil.

Since Termiz did not become the stepping stone to Afghanistan, I found myself full of doubts and questions. I now know God used the time to better equip me. The Spirit of God was schooling me in the subjects known as perseverance and patience. My character was still being developed. Endurance was becoming a way of life. I was learning that you can't grow weary in doing well, but must press on into greater maturity and faithfulness. God was teaching me to focus on living each day in His grace. I was discovering His joy as my strength. These were serious lessons for someone who was about to serve as "a flame on the front lines" in Northern Afghanistan.

Another gift was actually left on my lips. I did not realize it at the time and wouldn't discover its value until a year later. While I was teaching English to Uzbeks that year, they were teaching me the Uzbek language. My familiarity with that language turned out to be a key part of my work in Afghanistan. But I don't want to let the cat out of the bag. You will have to keep reading the book.

While I was still taking baby steps toward Afghanistan, God was working on me. The question was, "Could I rest in His all-wise plan even though I didn't know what it was?" Is that not what sovereignty means? He is God and we are not. He is calling the shots! *It is all about Him*. He is God alone, who knows everything and sees from the beginning to the end. His timing is perfect. He would one day give me the joy of living and working in Afghanistan at a strategic time in history. I was yet in training. In fact, I am still today. I was learning the hard way that God continues to prepare us all our lives. He is never done with us this side of eternity. We are all under construction.

During times of impatience (a major project area in my life), I've often been reminded of God's approach in the process with the Prophet Moses. Preparation Phase One for service involved 40 years of personal and academic development in Egypt. Phase Two took 40 years, in which Moses practiced leading people around the wilderness by leading sheep. Moses reached 80 before God revealed his main assignment. After all that, Moses carried on under God's continual preparation. I guess I've had it pretty easy after all.

Having to leave Termiz and then Uzbekistan did create tremendous disappointment for me. I was so close I could practically smell Afghanistan. I wondered if, like Moses, I was only going to gaze upon the land of my dreams from the far side of the river, without ever setting foot on its soil. I cried out to God: "What's happening here. What's the plan now?" I was hoping the border would miraculously open. Maybe the river would divide, and I would just walk over. The flame was still burning, but I wondered if I would ever shine inside Afghanistan.

# Chapter 9

# Regions Beyond

The summer of 1999 found me back at the Ponde-rosa in Weaverville. It was a delight to serve once more at Mt. Bethel FWB Church. Those were good months of ministry and strengthening relation-ships. I felt loved, supported, and encouraged. There were many opportunities to talk about my experi-ences and my vision. This kept my heart and my prayers focused on Afghanistan. Because God still had me "in a holding pattern," I began looking for a way to increase my teaching credentials. I decided to pursue a certificate in Teaching English as a Second Language (TESOL). That training would come in handy moving into new cultures.

In September 1999 I learned of a conference in Thailand that would involve many of the people, ministries, and agencies serving in Central Asia. In planning for this event, I also found a school in Thailand that offered the teaching course I wanted.

So I was off to Thailand to sharpen my skills as a teacher and gather with others to explore options for service in the "stans."

## Breathtaking Beauty

The first stop on my itinerary was Ban Phe, an exotic remote island that declared the glory of God's creation. I arrived there after Christmas of 1999 from Bangkok by bus. The school I would attend was Trinity Thailand, part of a larger institution in London. It offered the courses to earn a certificate to teach English. For me, it was another strategic step of preparation. My teaching ability was further polished. Again, I was reminded how much I love to teach.

As usual, a local family adopted me. Mr. Watcharin, the father, became a friend. He helped me adjust to Thai life and taught me how to play local sports. I had the time of my life with my new adopted family. Even the smallest efforts to learn someone's language can yield incredible results. Hearing a complete stranger speak your mother tongue touches your heart. Many Americans, however, assume others should learn English and, therefore, make little effort to learn foreign languages.

I could write a book about relationships that were formed simply because I greeted someone in his dialect. When I tried out a phrase on Mr. Watcharin at school one day, my few words in Thai released a flood of hospitality. He and his family invited me into their lives because I showed an interest in their language. That eventually allowed me to talk about the Lord Jesus, who will someday be praised in every language. Once again, God allowed me to participate in extending His blessings, this time Thai style.

## Divine Breakfast

Certificate in hand, I next flew north to Chiang Mai for a conference in February 2000. As I traveled I was trying not to be overly hopeful. I was prayerful and had questions like: "What will God say to me? Who will I meet there?" I did want to trust God and His wisdom that orchestrates the affairs of our lives. Yet would this be just another get-together of international workers?

God did arrange many divine appointments and strategic connections. A specific breakfast with two guys stands out the most. That morning, there had been a discussion on the details of humanitarian work inside Afghanistan. The international community had been focused primarily on providing emergency relief and immediate shelter for people left homeless by the civil war, drought and recent earthquakes. By the time we met at breakfast, there was a desire to discuss other long-term solutions that needed to be addressed. The organization, of these two men, was hoping to expand into areas of sustainable community development and educational programs.

While we three were talking, I remembered hearing about the earthquakes in Northern Afghanistan. My mind recalled meetings in Uzbekistan when we were praying for the victims and for those who could launch relief efforts. Some had even said, "John, this may be your chance." I did consider the possibility, but still had a commitment in Termiz at the time. Thus, I did not pursue it. I also remembered seeing images of the thousands of Afghan refugees on the Pakistani border and how some of my friends went to serve there.

My two breakfast companions had known about some of us in Uzbekistan and had made preliminary contacts to recruit for their emergency relief response in Afghanistan. An email had been sent from Tajikistan asking if anyone would "come over and help us." For some reason I, the zealous activist, was kept from responding. It was a good idea, but the wrong timing. God's hand restrained me from being impulsive.

A lot had changed since then, and now I was in Thailand, breaking bread with these two men, in a God-ordained moment. "Have you ever been to Afghanistan before?" They asked. "Do you still want to serve in Afghanistan?" Bells began to ring! I was in the right place at the right time. I told them I was ready to leave the next day. They said, "We need someone there immediately to teach English and pursue educational development. You could go tomorrow. We have an office there, but you would be responsible for starting the program." I dropped my spoon.

The door was finally open! I said I would need approval from the elders back at Mt. Bethel and the rest of my support team. I told them they would hear from me shortly. I flew back to the States, feeling as if I didn't need an airplane. My friends in Weaverville gave an enthusiastic blessing. Other supporters and counselors chuckled and said things like, "Well, it's about time!" I would soon leave for Tajikistan, since it was one of the countries with access to Afghanistan. The only way to get to Tajikistan was a weekly international flight from Munich, Germany, so my travels would soon turn me in the direction of Europe.

## London

My seven-year dream was about to come true. But there was one problem. I needed an entry visa, or official permission, for Tajikistan. Scheduling flights and buying tickets was a piece of cake, but I was still waiting for my Tajik visa application to be processed. In the States time ran out and I had to leave for London in July 2000. I had promised to take my sweet little sister, Sandi Lynn, and our dear niece, Connie, to London as part of their graduation present. Yes, I have an aunt who finished high school the same year my little sister did. It was great fun, from the tower of London, to Cheers, to bus rides, to Rockola Café. They keep me hopping, or bouncing as they liked to say. We had a blast! By the time they returned to the States, I needed some rest!

I did relax for a day before traveling around the UK to visit friends who have the same passion for kingdom work in the "stans." Reconnecting with many of them was refreshing. Then I took a short flight over to Holland to attend the Amsterdam 2000 Conference. This was a huge gathering for international Christian workers from all over the world. I witnessed an assembly of the main ethnic groups of over 200 countries. It was a foretaste of Heaven, for it reminded me of the promise that every people group will have representatives around the Throne of God.

Visualize it! What a day that will be when we hear the loud song, "Worthy is the Lamb, Who was slain, Who has redeemed us from every tribe, nation, kindred and tongue." Every hour for several days, I heard firsthand what God is up to on Planet Earth—remarkable stories. The Spirit of God is moving all over the world.

The Billy Graham Evangelistic Association sponsored that memorable event. Again, I was led back to all the stones of remembrance, especially that first time I heard the Good News of Jesus at Stafford High School. Those words, "For God so loved the world," still stirred my heart! I was overwhelmed one day, when in a crowd of thousands, I bumped into several friends I had previously met in the "stans." I do not recall meeting anyone from Afghanistan; however, I believed that at the next such gathering the Land of Afghans would have better representation.

After much spontaneous prayer and giving thanks, I said many good-byes. The week was like a fresh baptism of God's Spirit and a new anointing for me. I did not want to leave, but needed to journey on from Amsterdam to my next stop, Germany. Why? My application for a Tajik visa in the States had been denied, not once or twice, but three times. I still don't know why.

## Berlin

I trusted that while visiting some German friends, who support various works in Central Asia, God would give me another chance for a visa. I boarded a train from Amsterdam to Berlin, continually praying for the Father's favor. I remember reflecting, "How lovely it was to be in London with my sister and niece, and part of me wanted to pitch a permanent tent and dwell in His presence in Holland at Amsterdam 2000." I was so caught up in the moment that I almost forgot where I was and where I was going. Then it hit me, "What if I don't get a Tajik visa in Germany?"

I arrived in Berlin and was hosted by a gracious German family. They were known to help people called to serve in Central Asia. We prayed a lot together and shared how God had been working in our lives. They were excited about my plans to go to Afghanistan. I remember the day I traveled by subway to the Tajik Embassy. Martin and Andrea had two small children, so I took public transport in order not to burden them.

As I approached the Embassy I was nervous. I entered, introduced myself, and asked for a visa application to Tajikistan. An official gave me the forms, and I filled them out in the office. Then I was told to come back in an hour. I was willing to pay extra to expedite the process. I left to find a post office where I would write several letters. There are so many back in Weaverville who have been faithfully praying for me: the Hensley, Brown, Edwards, Rice, Buckner, Ponder, Honeycutt and Barnett families—I could have continued for days. Writing was always comforting and a good way to keep connected with those at the home front.

## Stamped!

An hour later I returned to the Tajik Embassy, more anxious than before. To my surprise the visa was ready—no questions, no hassles. The official handed me a bill for $150. As the official gave me the visa, I could see God's hand in this provision. This was His doing. Should I have ever doubted? He has always been faithful and on time. Soon I would be on my way to Munich, one step closer to Afghanistan.

Two days later I was on that same subway, this time to the airport for a flight to Munich. Though Tajikistan is no longer under the rule of communism, it is still not easy to access. In Munich I would catch that weekly flight to Tajikistan, a country that borders the place that had captured my heart and bid me come.

The closer I got to my destination, the less people looked like me. From every direction I could hear snatches of exotic languages. I was reminded of my time in Russia with the Gundorin family. I tried to say a few words in Russian to my seatmate, if only to be polite and respectful. Ten hours later I arrived safely in the mysterious, mountainous country, Tajikistan, which is home to nearly five million inhabitants. It would now be my dwelling place and a base from which to launch into Northern Afghanistan.

God provided a small apartment nearly identical to those I called home in Russia and every other "stan" where I had lived. He even gave me a refugee from Afghanistan as a roommate, who quickly enlightened me. His gripping story of fleeing from the Taliban was not only heartbreaking; it was a dramatic reminder of what millions of Afghans have suffered. We drank much tea and told many stories during our time together.

His life illustrated the words of the Messiah, "The devil has come to steal, kill and destroy" (John 10:9). This young man had been through so much, but by God's grace was still alive. He had not seen his mother, brother and sisters in years. For some time they did not know each other's whereabouts. Thank God for the other half of the story, which is the Good News that **Jesus came to give life more abundantly** (John 10:10). My first Afghan friend was a passionate follower of the Prince of Peace. And by a series of miracles, he was reunited with his mother and siblings in another country.

I met other international workers and started learning about the structure, nature and scope of their involvement in Central Asia. I began to impatiently chart my course into Northern Afghanistan, but would have to wait a few weeks before boarding the UN plane headed south. After all, I needed to get oriented and get over this new stomach bug (we call it the Central-Asian-Weight-Loss Program), or dysentery. I didn't have an Afghan visa yet, and my colleagues were trying to extend my Tajik visa into a one-year, multiple-entry one, so I could travel in and out of Afghanistan. There were good reasons to stay put.

## Goo-goo

Meanwhile, I was meeting with two language tutors. A Tajik lady helped me learn some basic Tajik and Uzbek. Tajikistan is full of Uzbeks, thanks to Stalin and the Russians, who divided the general area of Central Asia into separate countries. My other instructor, a man from Kabul, taught me simple Dari phrases. He insisted that I learn the alphabet, which was frustrating. I kept saying, "Babies don't learn the alphabet first. They learn to goo-goo and gaa-gaa before anything else." Unfortunately, my classes were less than ideal because they only lasted a few weeks. They abruptly ended when my director announced our first trip south.

What had been happening south of Tajikistan? Afghanistan had suffered unspeakable trials and decades of civil war. Years of drought showed no sign of ending. Herds died and farmers were driven from their parched lands. Cities swelled as desperate refugees fled the fighting and starvation. Millions crossed the borders into Pakistan and Iran. Then devastating earthquakes rocked Northern Afghanistan in 1998, causing thousands of roofs to collapse on innocent victims as they slept. More than 7,000 Afghans lost their lives, and over 50,000 homes were destroyed or left unsafe. One area, called Rostaq, was hit the hardest. Several areas were almost wiped off the map.

## Jihad

The people of Afghanistan have suffered more than their share of destruction and death. There are millions of Afghan refugees around the world and thousands still internally displaced. There are count-less landmines scattered around the country, contin-ually killing or maiming the innocent with their unannounced explosions. Thousands have been left for dead or are now handicapped.

In areas where famine stalks and drought abounds, widows and orphans survive by begging in the streets. Thousands barely survive cold winters living in tents or makeshift shelter. Many animals in the West live in better conditions. One in four chil-dren dies before the age of five. The average life expectancy is 46 years. Illiteracy is still widespread. The mentality and dignity of thousands of Afghans has been adversely affected, as over two million have died since the Russian invasion of 1979.

In the name of Allah, the Taliban seized control of Kabul by driving out President Rabbani in 1996. Then the Taliban began to enforce its strict Islamic code. Where was Osama bin Laden at this time? He was in Afghanistan waging violent Jihad. His plans for terrorism and spreading al-Qaeda cells and the Taliban's view of life were a match made in hell.

The world had been ignoring the political turmoil in the country. Most turned a deaf ear; however, in 1998 Afghanistan made worldwide news again when it was rocked by a series of massive earthquakes. This natural disaster focused the eyes of many on the critical needs primarily in the north. Since Massoud was based there, he also got much exposure. The media served as his opportunity to remind the world of the problematic presence of the diabolic duo, the Taliban and al-Qaeda.

I'm not sure how much the West was listening, but, some did respond to the growing humanitarian crisis. The compassion-based groups that were already working in neighboring Tajikistan didn't have to look far to take action. With staff available, building projects up and running, and an invitation from the Northern Alliance, led by Rabbani and Massoud, some came to respond to the emergency in the mountainous areas of the northeast.

Some brothers, who were serving in the Land of the Tajiks, flew from its capital, Dushanbe, into Northern Afghanistan to assess the situation. This was a first, as they flew into the war zone in a Russian helicopter. They saw plenty of AK-47's as soldiers of the Northern Alliance greeted them. Thankfully, these relief workers were not shot at, but were welcomed with open arms. They were the first Westerners to witness and survey the extensive earthquake damage.

As large an area as Central Asia is, outsiders tend to be a very obvious minority. Members of groups providing humanitarian assistance, for example, all know each other and try to coordinate their efforts. Because resources are limited, organizations have to decide whether to compete or cooperate. To meet the desperate needs in the area, cooperation is the best policy. Often, there's no other choice.

## Hope Reborn

The Christian organization that I then belonged to worked hard to gain the respect of other agencies by its practices, programs and willingness to serve others. We have often been able to place qualified staff in areas where others agencies could only transport significant amounts of relief materials. Agencies like USAID and the UN often have massive quantities of materials and huge international delivery systems, but rely on locally based distribution agencies that are familiar with a region. This assures that the relief gets to the people who need it most. At that time, as one of the only international organizations in the area, we served as a main implementer for most of the major donors like USAID, WFP and the UN.

As international workers became involved in responding to affected areas in the world, it became clear that once the critical needs have been met after a disaster or war, a new set of needs arises for the displaced. Should they return home? Should they settle permanently in a new location? If their homes have been damaged or destroyed by the elements or the fighting, what can be done to provide permanent housing? What should be done about disrupted schools, local government, bombed buildings, ongoing drought, destroyed or nonexistent water supplies, waste management, roads, and medical facilities? Survivors need sustained help to re-establish a place to call home.

Refugees need ongoing assistance in rebuilding their lives, hopes and dreams. They need help in creating a means to provide food for themselves and their families. They need established clinics, jobs, security, help with various facets of community development. They need life skills. Therefore, they needed organizations, such as ours, that could offer both immediate assistance as well as help for the long road of recovery and development.

With a better understanding of both the history of the need and some of the humanitarian responses, I was ready to take the next step. With visas in my passport, a UN plane ticket in my pocket, and a spring in my step, I eagerly anticipated seeing my new home first from the sky. An altitude of 20,000 feet barely gets you over some of the huge mountain ranges of the Hindu Kush. How breathtaking my flight would be and what a joy to finally set foot on the ground that was the place of my dreams! At this point I was fully aglow—a flame headed to the front line.

# Chapter 10

# Go Home

Solomon's proverb proved true: "Desire accomplished is sweet to the soul." My heart leaped as my feet landed on Afghan soil for the first time! There was deep satisfaction as my spirit sang a new song. I don't know which was more wonderful, the breathtaking view or the warm welcome. Being a "people person" who grew up mostly in the southern part of the United States, the friendly greetings made me feel right at home.

I had a bushy beard, which is the norm for Muslim men. I could also speak some Uzbek, which is often heard in Northern Afghanistan, and Dari, which is the Afghan version of Farsi spoken by over half the population. Perhaps they thought I was an Afghan who grew up in the West and was returning for the first time. Or the affectionate reception could have been because they were so indebted and appreciative of our humanitarian assistance. Reciprocity is a major part of Afghan culture.

I was impressed by Afghan hospitality and even gained a few pounds. Legend has it that Central Asian people wrote the book on how to entertain guests. A few Afghan proverbs illustrate this: "The guest is the friend of God" and "On the first day you meet as friends, the next as brothers." Most of us in the West could learn a lot from our Eastern friends. Even the Word of God tells us, "Don't forget to show hospitality to strangers, for some who have done this have entertained angels without realizing it!" (Hebrews 13:2).

One very important aspect of life that I soon noticed was daily interaction. Relationships are essential in Afghan culture. I enjoyed seeing the good-natured humor and friendliness among Afghan men. Every conversation included stories. My Afghan neighbors are exceptional communicators and very entertaining storytellers. This means there are at least two vital keys for making friends: a liking for drinking tea and telling or listening to stories.

**Long Legacy**

I prefer green tea and can tell pretty good stories. To my surprise, many enjoy listening to them. I am an amateur, however, compared to my Afghan colleagues, who are more gifted storytellers than I am. The "stans" have a long tradition of storytelling that dates back thousands of years. This is quite a legacy when you consider that most of them have never read or written anything in their lives.

Organizations like ours have worked hard in the education sector. We build schools for both boys and girls, provide teacher training and support, as well as necessary educational supplies. We have also distributed thousands of Operation Christmas Child gift boxes that share the season of joy and encourage students. In spite of the efforts of the entire international community, Afghanistan's literacy rate is still less than 50 percent. One factor might be that this part of the planet is an oral society. Picture this: You cannot read or write, but you can quickly tell hundreds of stories, perhaps in multiple languages and maybe even quote verbatim the Holy Quran in Arabic. This is true for millions in the Eastern world who have memorized volumes simply by listening with their two ears. Astonishing!

## Islam...Muslims

As you might have guessed, many of my friends are committed Muslims. To them being Muslim goes hand in hand with being Afghan, so if you are an Afghan, then you are a Muslim. Most of them have "Mohammed" or "Abdullah" in their name. Allah is the Arabic word for God, Mohammed is the beloved prophet of Islam and Abdullah (Abdul for short) is the Arabic word meaning "Slave of Allah." Islam is monotheistic. Muslims believe in one God, and that God is one, the Almighty, Most Merciful. They are very religious. Their faith is an all-encompassing worldview that permeates every aspect of their lives. Three of the most common Arabic phrases illustrate this: *Inshallah* (God willing), *Alhamdulillah* (Praise God), and *Bismillah* (In the name of God).

Muslims in every country, regardless of their mother tongue, know this religious lingo. They hear and say it hundreds of times a day. Devout Muslim men around the world might describe their daily life like this: "As I wake up I say *Alhamdullah* or *Bismillah* or a combination of both. Regardless of what my first activity is I invoke the name of Allah and give glory to God. I do this throughout the day and also in the evening before I sleep with my wife. Almost every time someone asks me a question I answer, *Inshallah*. We use these words over and over and even more when we go five times a day to the mosque, our place of worship. The call to prayer, which is chanted loudly five times a day in Arabic, not only invites every Muslim to bow in worship, but invokes the blessings of Allah and declares what we believe about Allah and his beloved prophet Mohammed, peace be upon him."

## Quit!

God deeply loves Afghans and all Muslims. Yet laboring among them is demanding. My Heavenly Father gave me a heart for Afghans, their culture and language. Since 2000, however, there have been many days when I wanted to give up. The challenge is enormous. All around were needy people, lost like sheep without a shepherd. Overwhelmed, overburdened and overworked, I considered going home.

Several times I tried to quit. I even rehearsed my resignation. But God was faithful. Remember, I believe God is the One Who ordained my destiny. He is the One Who gave me the vision. He is the One Who called me to work among Afghans. I could have thrown in the towel and left the land of my dreams, but the Hand of Providence restrained me.

The Bible says: "I thank Christ Jesus our Lord, who has given me strength to do His work. He considered me trustworthy and appointed me to serve Him, even though I used to blaspheme the name of Christ. In my insolence, I persecuted His people. But God had mercy on me because I did it in ignorance and unbelief. Oh, how generous and gracious our Lord was! He filled me with the faith and love that come from Christ Jesus." (I Timothy 1:12-14).

Afghanistan's extreme terrain and my daily surroundings often influenced my mood. God's majestic mountains inspired me; on the other hand the dry, dusty desert depressed me. Although generally a stable person, I did experience many highs and lows.

One day, at the end of my rope and in dire desperation, I cried out to God. I was lonesome, exhausted and discouraged. I wanted to return home to the States and get married. My residence was the guestroom in what we called the "greenhouse." We had rented this building in 2000 for our educational institute. It represented many of the reasons I came to Afghanistan. I remembered my TESOL training, teaching English and envisioning being a teacher among Afghans. (Years later this very room would be where my future wife and her friends would celebrate on the eve of our wedding.)

**Touched**

But God came through that day. He met me in the greenhouse. It was life-changing. He reminded me how He called me, guided me and provided for me all along the way. He reminded me of ways that He was at work, even if the process seemed slow and insignificant to me. Then He told me to listen to a well-known sermon by Dr. John Piper entitled "Doing Missions When Dying Is Gain." Part of me wanted to die, but I found the tape and did what I was told.

As I listened to the tape, my heart began to soften and my eyes shed tears. Cross-cultural living in a conservative Islamic society had been getting the better of me. My flame had almost flickered out. I nearly lost the vision and almost gave up. Something in my soul began to stir and burn deep within as I heard the timely message. The Spirit of God touched me anew. Again, I felt like "a flame on the front line." God gave me new resolve. I was determined that if it was God's will for me to be single, or even die in His service, I would still love and serve Him with all my heart.

That divine day, my soul sang a new song, "May You, Jesus, the Lamb Who was slain receive the reward of Your suffering." I resumed the battle full of faith and passion. I began to see how all our projects were opportunities to share His love in word and deed. We were His salt and light in the community. Like the leaven in the dough, the knowledge of His love was spreading. Our years of hard work were not in vain.

## Helpful Heroes

With renewed commitment, I rallied with our team of expatriates and Afghans to serve more effectively. It was daily spiritual warfare, but we were united in the cause. I must admit, though, I still struggled with being single. In the dry times, God used His Word and the stories of others like a cup of cold water. I camped out in the book of Psalms where King David continually pours his heart out to God. I reread the journals of Hudson Taylor. His pioneering and persevering life, especially the story of meeting his wife in China, cheered me on in the race I was running.

Also, knowing how William Carey responded to hardship and setbacks in his work in India with "By God's grace, I will keep plodding," caused me to press on. I am indebted to those at FWBBC who acquainted me with such legendary people of faith. Thank God for heroes and the great company of saints who have gone before us. As my Afghan friends would say, "Afarin," which means "Well done."

Or in the words of the Apostle Paul: "As for me, my life has already been poured out as an offering to God. The time of my death is near. I have fought the good fight, I have finished the race, and I have remained faithful. And now the prize awaits me—the crown of righteousness, which the Lord, the righteous Judge, will give me on the day of his return. And the prize is not just for me but for all who eagerly look forward to his appearing. (II Timothy 4:6-8).

*Forbidden Harvest*, by Dr. Christy Wilson, known as one of the apostles to Afghanistan, deeply inspired me. In the 70s, while I was still in diapers, he established the Christian Community Church of Kabul. Though the church building was later destroyed, he did not stop plowing and planting in the vineyard of the Lord. He was a flame who left us a magnificent legacy. Also, Gordon Magney, who pioneered solar work in Central Asia, spoke into my life several times. He was a wealth of resource and a great source of support to me. All of these brothers have run their race. They finished well.

The Bible says in Hebrews 12:1-2, "Therefore, since we are surrounded by such a huge crowd of witnesses to the life of faith, let us strip off every weight that slows us down, especially the sin that so easily trips us up. And let us run with endurance the race God has set before us. We do this by keeping our eyes on Jesus, the champion who initiates and perfects our faith. Because of the joy awaiting Him, He endured the cross, disregarding its shame. Now He is seated in the place of honor beside God's throne."

## Save Who?

I travel to the States almost every year, but I am not sure if it is home. Psalm 90 says, "Lord, through all generations You have been our home!" One of my favorite old hymns is "This world in not my home. I'm just passing through. My treasures are laid up somewhere beyond the blue. The angels beckon me from Heaven's open door and I can't feel at home in this world anymore." I love America and Afghanistan. I can live in either country; however, neither is actually home. My real citizenship is in Heaven with

Jesus. Maybe it is true that home is where your heart is, and that is why there is longing in my soul for our eternal home.

I thoroughly enjoy visiting family, friends and supporters while traveling to the States or other countries. A holiday break is regularly needed. This is a time to recharge, reconnect with fellow-worshippers and tell stories about life and work in Afghanistan. There are some fascinating conversations on these trips. On one visit, while eating dinner with friends, I was asked a question. That the inquirer was only eight years old made it more interesting and surprising. As I took another bite of chicken, I was not expecting young Stephan to say, "Mr. John, have you converted any Muslims over there?"

# Chapter 11

# Answering Abdullah

After learning language and earning respect, God often led me to ask Afghans thought-provoking questions. "Abdullah, what do you believe about Heaven?" This is one way to start a conversation. Because of their curiosity and interest, most discussions were initiated by Afghans. "John, are you a Christian?" or "Do you believe Jesus is the Son of God" or "Why do you know that you go to Heaven when you die?"

The Lord tells us to always be prepared to answer anyone who asks us about the hope that we have. In Afghanistan, we have discovered the best response to a question is an open-ended statement, a story or another question. If I quickly answer with "yes" or "no" there is little chance of investigating what Abdullah means or why is he asking. He might be trying to get me in trouble or seeking to find the Way. "Abdullah, what do you mean by saying 'Christian' or 'Son of God'?" This allows the chat to continue, builds a potential bridge in the dialogue, and creates a possible opportunity to plant seeds. Usually, this approach gave Abdullah something to chew on and discuss with his other friends.

## Casting Stones

One day I had been invited to drink tea with the mayor. He is one of the most influential men in the area for several reasons. First, he towers over others like Sampson or Goliath. He is over six and a half feet tall, which is huge for an Afghan. Second, he was a fierce and fearless mujahidin fighter and has many battle scars to prove it. Third, he is a relative of General Nazermat, who rules most of Northeastern Afghanistan. He appreciates and admires our work.

I look up to the mayor as a father or uncle, not just because he is so tall. Since we are friends and allies, he repeatedly includes me in the community gatherings. That day the topic was adultery, because there was a promiscuous woman in the neighborhood. The room was full of the elders of our district. Amazed to be sitting in the room, I sipped my tea and listened carefully to the story.

Suddenly, one of the gray-bearded mullahs (religious men) looked me in the eye and said, "Mr. John, we all know you are a follower of the Messiah. Do you believe a woman who commits adultery should be stoned to death? What does your Holy Book say?" Talk about being put on the spot. As I fumbled for words, I remembered it is always best to ask permission. So I scanned the eyes of the eager listeners in the room and asked, "Ijosa ast?" meaning "Is there permission?" After hearing several affirmative grunts, I said, "That is a good question and it reminds me of story in the Holy Book." As best I could in Dari, with God's help, I told the account of the woman caught in adultery in John 8.

You could have heard a pin drop. Perhaps you know about Jesus stooping down and silently scribbling in the sand, as a mob of men were angrily questioning Him about whether or not the Law of Moses commanded that the immoral woman be killed. (I always wondered why they did not ask the adulterous man about his unfaithfulness). Anyway, the often quoted one-liner of the Messiah hit them right between the eyes, "If any one of you is without sin, let him be the first to throw a stone at her." They had no stones to throw that day. Perchance some even had ears to hear the Loving Savior say, "Neither do I condemn you. Go now and leave your life of sin."

**Salvation**

Stephan's question at the dinner table that evening startled me, because for many reasons I feel uncomfortable using the word "conversion." Why? We cannot convert anyone. That is not our job. Salvation is from the Lord. The wages of sin is death, but the gift of God is eternal life through Jesus Christ our Lord. We have all sinned and fallen short of the glory of God. We are all in the same sinking boat. Guilty! Condemned! The Good News is Almighty God is the Most Merciful. He is slow to anger, rich in love and quick to forgive. But we can do nothing to receive

God's favor, except plead the blood of Jesus Christ to wash away our sins, and cover our shame.

The Bible says: "But God is so rich in mercy, and He loved us so much, that even though we were dead because of our sins, He gave us life when He raised Christ from the dead.....He raised us from the dead along with Christ and seated us with Him in the heavenly realms because we are united with Christ Jesus....God saved you by His grace when you believed. And you can't take credit for this; it is a gift from God. Salvation is not a reward for the good things we have done, so none of us can boast about it. For we are God's masterpiece. He has created us anew in Christ Jesus, so we can do the good things He planned for us long ago." (Ephesians 2:4-10).

Conversion is an act of God. Yahweh, the God of Abraham, Isaac and Jacob, promised to bless all the families of the earth. We don't convert anyone. Only God can cleanse the human heart. He is the One Who gives us new life. As co-laborers with God, we are called to share the Gospel, which is the power of God that saves all who believe. The results are in God's hands. Some plant, some water, but God is in charge of the garden.

It is true that millions of followers of the Messiah all over the world have a "conversion story." The word conversion, however, has a negative tone in most places. In many religious circles, like Hinduism, Judaism, Islam, and Buddhism, which make up half the population of the planet, you are disowned or even killed if you convert to another religion. This is partly due to the fact that cultural and religious identity goes hand in hand in the Eastern world. Becoming a Christian, however, is coming to know the Lord Jesus in a personal way, not necessarily abandoning one's culture or "changing religions."

The call to follow Christ is not an invitation to become Western. Democracy is not the answer. Jesus is the King of kings and Lord of lords. He is the hope of the nations and the Savior of the World, Who is the solution to the problem of sin and death. Those of us involved in cross-cultural ministry must be very careful to separate culture from God's eternal truth.

For example, where does the Bible teach believers to wear suits and ties, sit on pews and sing from hymn books, and listen to a man speak loudly from a black book every Sunday morning at 11:00am? I think you get the point that this is only one cultural way of doing church. It is neither wrong nor right. If a group of Muslims gather on Friday and kneel in the direction of Jerusalem to worship the Messiah that is fine, too. The forms and styles of worshipping the One True Living God may vary all over the world.

## Christ or Culture

It is understandable, in working cross-culturally, if there is conflict over the teaching about Jesus dying on the Cross. The Bible speaks about the Cross being an offense to some, but the power of God that saves others. Yet sometimes the clash of cultures is the result of how the Gospel of Jesus is packaged. Sometimes it comes as a nice Western Christmas present, where you must attend church with a steeple on Sunday morning, sing songs translated from English, and pray with hands crossed and eyes closed. We who share the Gospel have to disconnect ourselves from our home culture or religious experience. As Jesus humbled Himself and became man, we, too, must lay aside self and learn both language and culture to communicate appropriately. This is what the Apostle Paul meant by, "becoming all things to all people."

Most of what and how we practice faith is formed by our culture. Yet no one culture is better than another. There are traces of the divine in every culture, although, none leads directly to God, not even Western culture. The Lord Jesus Christ alone is the Way, the Truth and the Life. The essence of Christianity is not a religious system, but a loving, obedient relationship with Almighty God the Creator and Heavenly Father of all those who believe in the Lord Jesus Christ. The Messiah is the only One sent from God, Who died on a Cross and rose again from the dead to conquer death, defeat the devil, destroy the power of sin and prove He is the Son of God.

It doesn't matter if you are American, Jewish, Arab, Palestinian, Indian or Afghan. Anyone can come to know the Lord anywhere. Yes, this frequently happens in a public place of worship, but God doesn't live in a building. The Lord is still mighty to save sinners in a prison in Alcatraz, a pub in England, a mosque in Afghanistan, a penthouse in Hollywood or the privacy of your own home. It doesn't matter who we are or where we are. As we sing with our children, "Red and yellow, black and white they are precious in His sight, Jesus loves the little children of the world."

God created us and desires us for Himself. It is His Spirit Who convicts us of our need for salvation and draws us with His cords of kindness. He is the wonderful Wooer of Adam's race. It is His goodness that brings us to repentance. Whenever or wherever the Spirit of God illuminates or gives revelation, as if God is calling our name, we can call on the Name of the Lord Jesus and be saved. This miracle is known as spiritual rebirth. As a result, the Spirit of God takes up residence in us. He makes His home in our hearts. Our spirit becomes one with God's Spirit. He dwells among His sons and daughters, for He promises to be wherever two or three gather in His Name.

## The 11th Hour

God is at work inside Afghanistan. Jesus said, "My Father is always working, and so am I." The Spirit of God is moving all over the Muslim world. The Lord God says: "In the last days, I will pour out my Spirit on all people. Your sons and daughters will prophesy, your young men will see visions, your old men will dream dreams." Jesus is passionately pursuing His beloved bride from every tribe, nation, kindred and tongue. His love is so real that when touched by it, we not only want to love Him in return, but are compelled to share it.

A treasured story of this is from one of my favorite persons on the planet, Abdul Jon. He grew up in a family of farmers. Like most young Afghan men, fate led him to the military, where he served as a mechanic. I remember the day we met. I can still see the passion in his eyes. How shocked I was when he asked, "May I tell you how I came to know the Messiah?" What a surprising question from an Afghan, and, oh, what an answer of the redeeming love of the Desire of Nations! I wish we were sitting face-to-face, so I could tell you the rest of the story. Only God knows, but maybe there are millions of Muslims around the world who worship the Messiah.

## Honeymoon

Remember that beautiful woman? I met her, the woman of my dreams, in Afghanistan. It was a match made in Heaven. We fell in love riding a bicycle together on the busy streets of Kabul. As unusual as it might sound, we tied the knot in Afghanistan. God gave us the honor of uniting in marriage in the land of our dreams. Even more unusual, the Land of the Afghans is where my American wife, Jeanne, was born. In some ways she is even more committed than I am to the work among Afghans.

Through our week-long wedding celebrations, God allowed us to give His Word to over a thousand Afghans. A year later, Jeanne gave birth to our first child in Kabul, not far from where she entered the world. With two family members having Afghanistan written as "place of birth" in their passports, I am bound for life to "the call" to serve Afghans. Oops, this story is for Chapter 12 or maybe another book called *Najiba*, my wife's Afghan name.

God sent my wife, Jeanne, back to the land of her birth. He did so from New York City. Now, being married to Jeanne, counts for virtually 7,000 reasons to continue serving in Afghanistan. At Times Square Church every Sunday thousands of passionate believers gather "like a great multitude of all nations, people and languages." It is the church that God's love is building.

Also, on Thursday nights nearly 700 believers join together at the church to pray for the needs of the nations. They believe God shapes the world through prayer. Talk about mighty intercession and heavenly agreement. They frequently remember us by name. Their motto is "every voice counts" as they worship King Jesus and call upon the Name of the Lord. We are grateful for this strategic partnership in the Big Apple, or New York City, and the monthly orphanage support of Child Cry, an international feeding program sponsored by Times Square Church.

Our cozy honeymoon home, nestled in the mountains of Northeastern Afghanistan, had few creature comforts. We had a floor mattress, a gas stove, a wood heater and an outhouse. I was the running water, as I fetched it daily in a bucket from the water tap we installed on our neighborhood street. Our humanitarian projects were designed to improve the quality of life for Afghans, yet even the benefit of this spring water project reached into our house.

Having lived in this remote area and being a simple guy from the southern part of the United States, I was overwhelmed the first time Jeanne took me to Times Square in New York City. Wow, look at all the electricity, so many sounds and sights and lights! I read every billboard. Times Square has some remarkable ones, maybe the best in the world. My favorite billboard was from the "Pass It On" series entitled *Devotion*. It shows a photo of the father-son Team Hoyt, with the caption, "65 marathons and still behind the wheelchair." God has used engaging testimonies like this to stimulate me and continually echo in my mind, "John, keep running the race. Never give up!"

**To Be or Not To Be?**

Though I did not grow up in a family of fellow worshippers, I am grateful for my limited Christian heritage and those God used to disciple me. Without the foundation I received at FWBBC, I don't know where I would be today. Those formative years have anchored and sustained me in the storms of life. In the last few years, God has led me down the "nondenominational or interdenominational" road. I am comfortable with phrases like "Free Will Baptist" or "Pentecostal," but don't like the labels we often wear as Christians. It is not important if you are "charismatic" or "evangelical." The main issue is not that of orthodoxy, or Catholicism or conservative theology. There are no perfect Christians this side of eternity. There is one God and Father of all. Jesus is Lord. He is Head of the Church, His Body. Jesus has One Beloved Bride, all those who are bought by His blood. If we belong to the Savior, we are brothers and sisters.

Serving in Afghanistan where there is no established church, I find it more honoring to God to simply unite around the fundamentals of our faith. Instead of viewing Christianity as a denomination or stressing one particular doctrine, I prefer to discover balance in God's eternal truth. Leading teams that have over 12 nationalities forces me to be inclusive and embrace others with grace. It might be harder and more challenging, but there is great reward in endeavoring to keep the unity of the Spirit. Working cross-culturally on a color-blind team helps me have more of God's heart and heavenly perspective. Keeping everything in its proper context and a commitment to unity are essential for Kingdom Work.

## Make a Difference!

Where we live is not the issue. You do not have to pack your bags and head to Afghanistan, but you should be willing to. If He leads you in this direction, you are welcome to stay and drink tea with us. The Spirit of God, Who dwells in us, desires to use each of us. He offers a fresh anointing in this 11th hour. He is like a consuming fire that longs to burn within us and set us ablaze with the beauty of our Lord Jesus Christ.

We are all God's flames. It doesn't matter who you are. You might be a pastor, a postman, a plumber. Maybe you are a housewife or a mother. Perhaps your calling is to be a doctor, a dentist, a nutritionist. On the front line of your life you are a flame! You could be a "Tyler" for a troubled teenager or an "Aunt Rena" who transforms an entire family or the next "Billy Graham" who influences whole nations. You are the light of the world. Let your light so shine before others that they might see your good works and glorify your Father who is in Heaven. Shine, I say, shine!

Perhaps you read *Kabul 24* or *Escape from Kabul*. Georg, our international director, is a modern-day flame and mentor in my life. The Lord led him to restart the work of Shelter Now in the early 90's after fundamentalists destroyed it in Pakistan. Against all odds, he took the risky step of faith. God gave him four important principles to govern the new work: a clear goal or kingdom focus, a team approach, a commitment to prayer and worship, and strategic projects to meet the felt needs of Afghans.

During his prison experience in 2001, it was the daily practice of prayer and worship that sustained Georg and the seven other Shelter Now workers. Although, the Taliban totally destroyed Shelter Now Afghanistan, God made a way for Georg and others to return to Kabul in 2002. It is great working along-side others who have endured such trials and are full of life experience.

Today, our Shelter Now Afghanistan staff is making a difference. God is blessing us and using us to bless Afghans. Lives are being changed and hope is being restored through our efforts. These include literacy, community development, water and sanitation, dental assistance, agriculture, small businesses, deaf centers, micro-finance, help for orphans and widows, animal restocking, educational endeavors, winter relief, and factories that produce concrete building materials.

## The Work Continues...

The Taliban and al-Qaeda are still around. After eight long years the military forces are still actively pursuing justice and promoting peace. Recently, the front page of *The Washington Post* read, "Marines Deploy on Major Mission: Thousands Fan Out in Afghanistan's South in Crucial Test for Revised U.S Strategy." The first line of the article says, "Thousands of U.S. Marines descended upon the volatile Helmand River valley in helicopters and armored convoys early Thursday, mounting an operation that represents the first large-scale test of the U.S. military's new counterinsurgency strategy in Afghanistan. The operation will involve about 4,000 troops from the 2nd Marine Expeditionary Brigade, which was dispatched by President Obama to combat a growing Taliban insurgency in Helmand and other southern provinces."

Those of us serving in Afghanistan have our work cut out for us. After celebrating 25 years of God's faithfulness to our organization, my family and I, together with the many other Shelter Now workers are still sharing God's love in word and deed. It is an honor to be "a team of flames on the front line." Compassion continues and so does the story...